Drawings by the Galli Bibiena Family

Eighteenth-Century Scenic and Architectural Design

DRAWINGS BY THE GALLI BIBIENA FAMILY

•

FROM COLLECTIONS IN PORTUGAL

Maria Alice Beaumont

ART SERVICES INTERNATIONAL
ALEXANDRIA, VIRGINIA

22 July–2 September 1990
Nelson-Atkins Museum of Art
Kansas City, Missouri

25 September 1990–1 January 1991
Cooper-Hewitt Museum
New York, New York

19 January–24 February 1991
Meadows Museum
Dallas, Texas

30 March–12 May 1991
Frick Art Museum
Pittsburgh, Pennsylvania

25 May–7 July 1991
The Octagon
Washington, D.C.

The exhibition was organized and is circulated by
Art Services International, Alexandria, Virginia.

Support for the exhibition has been provided by the Fundação Calouste Gulbenkian; the Luso-American Development Foundation, Lisbon; the American Portuguese Society, Incorporated; and the Banco Espirito Santo e Comercial de Lisboa. Additional support toward the production of the catalogue has been provided by The Andrew W. Mellon Foundation. TAP Air Portugal is the official carrier for the exhibition.

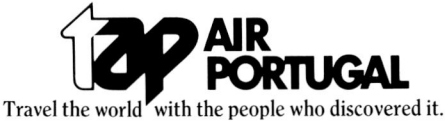

Travel the world with the people who discovered it.

BOARD OF TRUSTEES

Lynn Kahler Berg	DeCourcy E. McIntosh	Mrs. John A. Pope
James M. Brown, III	Mrs. Richard Mellon	Joseph W. Saunders
Jean C. Lindsey	Robert D. Papkin	Baroness Francesca Thyssen-Bornemisza

Copyright © 1990 by Art Services International, Alexandria, Virginia
All rights reserved

ISBN 0-88397-094-5

EDITOR: Nancy Eickel   DESIGNER: Stephen Kraft   TYPESETTER: BG Composition, Inc.
PRINTER: South China Printing Co. (1988) Ltd.

Cover illustration: Giovanni Carlo Bibiena, *Opera L'Olimpiade*, *Act 2, Scene 1*, pen and ink, pencil and sepia wash (cat. no. 60)

Printed in Hong Kong

Contents

Acknowledgments
7

Introduction
9

"Drawings by the Galli Bibiena:
Architecture and Scenography"
Maria Alice Beaumont
11

Checklist of Works
89

Bibliography
93

Acknowledgments

Nearly two hundred fifty years ago, as today, operas and theatrical performances served to stimulate the senses and stir the soul. European audiences from Bologna to Lisbon, from Vienna to Nancy, were led to extraordinary flights of imagination when attending performances held in theaters designed by Francesco Bibiena or when viewing fantastic operatic sets created by his son Giovanni Carlo Sicinio Bibiena. These and other members of the exceptionally gifted Bibiena family defined the standard for theatrical productions to which we are accustomed today. This exhibition provides the opportunity to appreciate the talent of the Bibiena family through their remarkable drawings.

It has been an honor to work with Dra. Maria Alice Beaumont, Director of the Museu Nacional de Arte Antiga in Lisbon and Guest Curator of the exhibition. She made the final selection of works and has generously shared her considerable scholarship with us. We have been continually impressed by her enthusiasm, and we thank her particularly for her devotion to this project.

We are grateful to both Dra. Beaumont and Professor Ayres de Carvalho, President of the Academia Nacional de Belas-Artes, for lending the outstanding works in this exhibition for tour. While the pieces will surely be missed in Portugal, they will be greatly valued and enjoyed during their brief stay in the United States.

We are privileged that Ambassador João Eduardo Monteverde Pereira Bastos has agreed to serve as Honorary Patron for this important exhibition, and we send him our thanks for his support. It is also a pleasure to acknowledge Graça Almeida Rodrigues, Cultural Counselor of the Embassy of Portugal, for her attention to this project.

It is with the greatest pleasure that we extend our heartfelt thanks to Phyllis C. Kane, our representative in Portugal. She has been our right arm, and her keen eye and untiring efforts have ensured the success of this endeavor.

Furthermore, we are indebted to the Fundação Calouste Gulbenkian and the Luso-American Development Foundation, Lisbon, for their support of this project. Once again we extend our appreciation to The Andrew W. Mellon Foundation, and notably to Neil L. Rudenstine, Executive Vice President, for its continued funding of our catalogue program. We also gratefully acknowledge the support of the American Portuguese Society, Incorporated, and the Banco Espirito Santo e Comercial de Lisboa, as well as Michael Teague for his invaluable assistance.

With great pleasure we announce that TAP Air Portugal is the official carrier of the exhibition. We especially recognize Eduardo Barbeiro, General Manager USA, for making this support possible.

The directors and coordinating curators of the museums on the national tour have been both encouraging and cooperative. Our warm thanks go to Marc F. Wilson and George L. McKenna at the Nelson-Atkins Museum of Art in Kansas City; Dianne H. Pilgrim and Dorothy T. Globus at the Cooper-Hewitt Museum in New York City; Donald E. Knaub and Maria Munoz-Blanco at the Meadows Museum in Dallas; DeCourcy E. McIntosh and Alan Fausel at the Henry Clay Frick Foundation and Frick Art Museum in Pittsburgh; and Nancy E. Davis and Judith S. Schultz at The Octagon in Washington, D.C. Their early support of this project ensured its successful development.

It has been a pleasure to collaborate once again with Nancy Eickel and Stephen Kraft on the production of this catalogue. They have handled the editing and design with considerable skill and creativity, and we thank them for sharing their talents with us.

Finally, we congratulate the staff of Art Services International, notably Marcene Edmiston, Elizabeth Hooper, and Sally Thomas, for their dedication and for seeing to the myriad details of the tour.

LYNN KAHLER BERG
Director

JOSEPH W. SAUNDERS
Chief Executive Officer

Introduction

Among the drawings in the Museu Nacional de Arte Antiga is an important collection of images of theaters, scenery, and other illustrations of architecture and decoration, all related to the eighteenth-century family of Italian scene designers, the Galli Bibiena. These artists, architects, and scenographers worked for several royal courts in Europe, building theaters and designing stage sets for operas and court festivities.

As a scholar and the founder of the dynasty, the first and most important member of the family was Ferdinando Bibiena. Although remarkable works were produced by the first and second generation of his descendants, no less significant are the accomplishments of his brother, Francesco Bibiena, whose son, Giovanni Carlo, was invited by King Joseph I to work at the Portuguese court, where he remained until his death. Included among the other works of scenography and architecture that Giovanni Carlo produced in Portugal is the Royal Opera House, which is especially noteworthy since it was the first one of its kind built in Lisbon. His achievement, however, was short-lived, for the theater was destroyed in the great earthquake of 1755, only seven months after its opening. Despite a lack of substantial documentation, the logical origin of the drawings in the Museu Nacional is the estate of Giovanni Carlo, particularly because numerous drawings by his father are included in this group.

While there are many collections of Bibiena drawings in museums in Europe and America, the holdings of the Museu Nacional de Arte Antiga rank among the most important remnants of the work of these famous Italian scene designers and architects. For this exhibition, our work goes no further than the critical use of existing sources and studies of the Galli Bibiena family. A few hypotheses that seem credible have been added, but the field is still open to further investigation.

Nevertheless, this presentation of drawings from the Bibiena collection in the Museu Nacional will provide an opportunity for these outstanding works of art to become known in America. In addition, it will allow them to be studied in relation to other collections of Bibiena drawings, such as those in the Cooper-Hewitt Museum and the Metropolitan Museum of Art, both in New York City, and the McNay Institute in San Antonio, Texas. It is with great pleasure and pride that we at the Museu Nacional offer this selection of works by Francesco and Giovanni Carlo Bibiena and other members of their family to audiences in the United States.

M. A. B.

Drawings by the Galli Bibiena Family: Architecture and Scenography

MARIA ALICE BEAUMONT
Director, Museu Nacional de Arte Antiga

Since the seventeenth century, and particularly in the eighteenth century, the common human tendency of dramatizing important social and private events has been strongly emphasized. Great religious, social, and political acts or popular feasts, such as Carnival and outstanding dates in the life of a well-known personality, became the pretext for creating stage settings filled with fiction and wonder. Characteristics most sought after for these feasts were dazzlement and mystery. If the term is allowed, which is after all enlightening, these feasts could be called funereal, since they involved both the passion of Christ and the earthly end of mortals. The mutations of scenographic visions that took place in some churches during Holy Week, or the pompous magnificence of the biers within the transcendental mystery of death and resurrection, contained the two essential elements of dazzlement and mystery. Yet even when the spectacles corresponded more literally to actual feasts, the characters often were kings, princes, or great lords—both metaphorically or in reality. Remember, for example, the participation of Louis XIV in a ballet in which he played the role of Apollo, or that of the Duchess of Lorraine and her daughters dancing in Lully's opera *Theseus*.

For the ultimate spectacle of opera, acted with or without pretext, many beautiful theaters were built. Court theaters, royal theaters, and communal and popular theaters with no entrance fee appeared in all parts of Europe that had any kind of theatrical tradition. In Lisbon, the predilection for spectacular feasts was common, although there was a clear separation between the periods of kings John V and Joseph I. The former era was marked by great liturgical pomp, whereas the latter displayed real fascination with operatic performances, which reached their peak with the creation of the short-lived Real Opera do Tejo. The marriages of John V and Joseph I brought to Portugal two princesses, both of whom came from families that manifested a strong interest in operatic theater and had members of the Bibiena family in their service.

The first princess, Marianne of Austria, daughter of Emperor Leopold I and sister of Emperor Charles VI (cat. no. 1), came from the court of Vienna. There, Francesco Bibiena rebuilt the Hoftheater, while Ferdinando and Giuseppe Bibiena were the scenographer-architects of Charles VI. Mariana Victoria of Bourbon, the wife of Joseph I, was granddaughter of Eduardo Farnese and Sophia Dorothea of Neuburg, the dukes of Parma, who were so influential to the careers of the two Bibiena brothers, particularly Ferdinando. Music and opera were thus ingrained in the cultural habits of these queens, and the name Bibiena would have been familiar to them.

In European courts of the eighteenth century, these theatrical and operatic productions often complemented essential episodes in the princes' lives. Birth, marriage, coronation, and official visits were accompanied by dramatizations of real or apparent happiness. Diplomatic missions used these displays to increase the prestige of their sovereigns. The requisite fantasy of these spectacles involved great sums of money as well as numerous agents, who worked to obtain the best performers, and a crowd of *virtuosi*—from scenographers, architects, prop men, and painters to the composer (such as Lully, Vivaldi, or Mozart), the librettist, singers, actors, and dancers. Although dazzling productions took place in galleries and palace gardens, it was indeed on stage and behind it that art, imagination, and ingenuity were most greatly exercised.

The eighteenth century also brought with it novelty and above all, many improvements. The theater or opera hall was treated, as beautifully as possible, as an acoustical box. Everything was studied: shape, size, facings (with particular attention directed toward the choice of wood), and the roof, with its devices for ventilation and sound conditioning. The deep stage contained machinery that, although heavy, was lighter than that of the previous century and was designed to surprise audiences with celestial apparitions and ingenious fire and water effects.

Certain rigid traditional conventions of renaissance scenery were abandoned, which allowed for multiple points of view, central as well as "per angolo." The latter was just an incipient idea before the time of Ferdinando Bibiena, but he developed, theorized, and applied the "per angolo" scene to such an extent that it can well be considered his innovation.

Parts of the stage scenery were made of painted canvas backdrops, and parts of the foregrounds were built with painted and gilded wood and plaster. The illusions of perspective forced the actors to stay far enough away from the background scenery to avoid aberrations in the comparative relationship between their height and that of the painted buildings or landscapes. Lighting required the same attention, since the disproportion of shadows could lead to absurd effects. Everything was examined in detail and professionally planned. Of interest here is the physical framework, both static and dynamic, of spectacles such as opera.

For about a century, more or less from 1680 to 1780, the Galli Bibiena family from Italy dominated the production of these elaborate feasts in Europe, designing both still and moving visual illusions for theaters. While they were not the only family to do so, these scenographer-architects were the most famous and the most sought after artists in their profession.

The family was originally from Florence, where they were known by the name "Galli." A certain Galli was appointed "podestá" of Bibiena (governor of its fortress). His descendant, Giovan Maria Galli, a painter who worked with Francesco Albani, added "da Bibiena" to the patronymic, and this soon became the second family name.

The sons of Giovan Maria Galli—Ferdinando (1657–1743) and Francesco (1659–1739)—and their descendants formed a family art business known for its cohesive technical and stylistic expression. Although each member of the family manifested his own personality, the work retained a strong unity, which makes it difficult to identify pieces on the basis of individual "style." Furthermore, much of the scenery that might be considered specific to a scene in a particular opera was most likely used as an adaptable prototype that circulated among family members, their collaborators, and their workshops. This typical Italian phenomenon of the family business, still visible today in the fields of finance and industry, elevated Ferdinando to a patriarch. Besides being the oldest and most famous family member, he had several children and grandchildren who followed in his footsteps, thanks to his work, books (cat. nos. 8–10), and teaching activity at the Academia Clementina.

Throughout his long life, Ferdinando Bibiena completed many commissions in Italy and abroad, which involved extensive travel even when he settled in Parma or Bologna. For Bibiena family members, Bologna was their fatherland. They were highly distinguished there, and they returned there to teach and to reinforce their unity. Thus, their meeting in Bologna in January 1744 became a memorable date in the family history. As others have suggested, the very architecture of the city, with its typical arcades, may have influenced the recurring shapes in Bibiena sceneries.

Francesco, born in Bologna in 1659, two years after his brother Ferdinando, had a long, laborious, and hectic life. Notices of his studies, work, and travels exist from at least 1672 until 1738. (He died the following year in Bologna.) From their first year of apprenticeship and work, the careers of the two brothers shared much in common. Francesco learned to paint and applied himself to frescos and *quadrattura*. He decorated many palaces and churches in Italy. The first significant references to his activity as a scenographer date from 1690, when he worked with his brother for the *teatrino di corte* in the duchy of Parma. From 1687 on, his brother Ferdinando remained in the exclusive service of the dukes, unable to accept other commissions without their consent. Francesco, however, enjoyed a mobility that seemed more temperamental than accidental. In 1738, at the age of seventy-nine, he traveled to Nancy to attend the marriage of one of his numerous children.

Having no strict responsibilities like his brother, Francesco undertook work in several cities when he was sent by the dukes Ranuccio and Odoardo Farnese or even by his brother Ferdinando. In 1702, at the invitation of the viceroy of Spain in Naples, Francesco supervised the celebrations surrounding the visit of Philip V, but he seems to have declined an invitation to go to Madrid. His work as a theatrical architect and scenographer was already well known and the family name of Bibiena was famous when Francesco was called to Vienna by Emperor Leopold I to rebuild the Hoftheater there. Although the theater opened in 1704, all that remains of it are a few drawings, with one of them, that of the stage curtain, now belonging to the Museu Nacional de Arte Antiga. A similar fate befell another famous work of his, the Nancy Opera, which was destroyed through several disasters. The few drawings that still remain of it (cat. nos. 32–39) are among the best of the museum's collection, and they testify to variations in the plan and to the progress of the project.

When the Hoftheater in Vienna was finished, Francesco returned to Italy for a short period. In 1707, he traveled to Lorraine at the invitation of Duke Leopold and Isabelle Charlotte, for whom he worked on the sceneries of temporary theaters in Lunéville and Einville. His great work there was the Nancy Opera, which opened in November 1709. From its commission to its inauguration and throughout its history, this theater has been sufficiently documented to serve as an enlightening example of what creating a princely opera house entailed. Along with François-Georges Pariset's publication on the opera house, the detailed study of Michel Antoine is indispensable, not only for its biography of Francesco Bibiena and the history of the theater in question, but also for its documentation on Bibienesque royal theater. This is especially important to scholars in Portugal, for much about the Bibienas' construction in Lisbon can be determined from the Nancy Opera.

Changes in the Nancy Opera project are visible in the four groups of drawings that still exist in the Lorraine Museum, the Louvre, the Metropolitan Museum of Art, and the Museu Nacional de Arte Antiga. Michel Antoine distinguishes those in Lisbon for being the most elaborate within the adopted version. Those in Nancy correspond to the first (abandoned) project, and those in Paris to a less-refined replica of the drawings in Lisbon. Pariset and Antoine compared Francesco Bibiena's work in Vienna and Nancy, and both concluded that the artist was stylistically influenced by the German baroque and French classicism. The drawings for the Nancy Opera are lighter and exhibit a simpler decoration. Bibiena was familiar with French taste not only in the Lorraine court, which at the time of his arrival was on favorable terms with Louis XIV, but also in Paris, which, according to Pariset, he visited at least once. Nancy was also the site of Francesco's 1709 marriage to the daughter of a court official whose responsibilities included the ducal tapestry workshop, for which Francesco made several cartoons. The bride, Anne Mitté, was sixteen and Bibiena fifty, although he said he was only forty.

At the end of that year he was recalled to Vienna by Emperor Joseph I, who was succeeded by Charles I two years later. The favor of the Austrian court then shifted to Ferdinando Bibiena, who had served the new emperor while he was still Charles III of Spain. Ferdinando and his sons even staged the prince's marriage party in Barcelona.

Francesco returned to Italy in 1713 and settled in Bologna, but he continued to travel frequently wherever commissions took him. Beautiful examples of architectural projects he designed for his own house (cat. nos. 40–46) are now in the collection of the Museu Nacional. The family crest of lilies and roosters (*galli* in Italian), and captions on the drawings support the attribution. The curators of the Bibiena exhibition held in Bologna offered some enlightening notes about these drawings. J.M. da Silva Correia identified them based on the graphic and architectural style of the undisputed drawings for the Nancy Opera.

Within this collection are drawings for a *palazzino* in Mantua (cat. no. 47) and the altars (now disappeared) of the Church of the Holy Spirit in Bologna (cat. no. 55). They form part of a group of projects (cat. nos. 50–54) for decorating as yet unidentified churches that were probably among the many in which Francesco Bibiena worked. His substantial production as a theatrical architect includes, in addition to theaters in Vienna and Nancy, the Aurora in Cento, the little theater of Rimini, and with particular importance, the Philharmonic Theater of Verona. The Alibert in Rome was created in collaboration with his nephew António. He also undertook several other projects in architecture, scenography, and decorative painting. Like his brother, Francesco was a professor at the Academia Clementina, and between 1727 and 1735 he frequently served as director of the faculty of architecture. When he died in 1739, he left a manuscript ready for printing that had the curious title *L'Architettura maestra delle arte che la compongono* (Architecture as master of the arts that compose it).

Francesco Bibiena and Anne Mitté had several children—Giuseppe, Giovanni Carlo Sicinio, Ludovico Antonio, Francesco Maria, and Rosa—but only one of them, Giovanni Carlo, followed in his father's profession. Born in Bologna on 11 November 1717, Giovanni Carlo Sicinio was christened in the church of San Biagio. His godfather was Count Sicinio Pepoli, from whom he must have received his third name. Giovanni Carlo spent the last eight years of his life in Portugal and died at the age of forty-three in Lisbon on 3 October 1760, the very year he became a Portuguese national. (We were able to sketch a biography of the artist by adding to material we already possessed and to data referred to by Deanna Lenzi and obtained by Ayres de Carvalho.)

Giovanni Carlo completed his technical and artistic studies in his hometown at the same Academia Clementina at which his father and uncle were distinguished teachers. He was twice considered the best student by the faculty of architecture, and he won the Marsili Award, which essentially secured his future career. In 1742, at the age of twenty-five, he joined the staff of the Academia Clementina and was appointed director of the faculty of architecture. He assumed this position again in 1745, 1746, 1749, 1750, and 1751. Giovanni Carlo married Isabella Beccari in Bologna in 1745. All that is known of her is that she was eight years his senior and that she died in Lisbon. They had three children—Anna, Teresa, and Giovanni Crisostomo. When they moved to Portugal, only the boy, then two years old, went with them. The girls, five and six years old, stayed with their uncles, the doctors Ludovico Antonio and Francesco Bibiena, according to the *Stade d'anime della parochia di San Biagio, per anno.*

Final arrangements for Giovanni Carlo's move to Portugal were negotiated through Nicolau Piaggio, the Portuguese consul in Genoa. The Bibiena family must have arrived in Portugal between 1751, when their names were still listed in the *Stade d'anime . . .*, and 1752, when they no longer appeared there. His first work in Lisbon was the improvisation of a theater in the Embassies' Room of the Ribeira Palace. Its opening on 12 September with the opera *Il Siroe* demonstrated Giovanni Carlo's imagination and competence. This served as a prelude for greater architectural and scenographic works.

Giovanni Carlo designed three theaters in Portugal, a palace with a chapel, and a church, which was begun shortly before his death. The first theater, that of the Salvaterra Palace, opened on 21 January 1753 during the winter season and was dedicated to hunting and music, since the king and the court traditionally spent this period in Salvaterra de Magos. Operas were also performed there during Carnival. Little has been known of this theater, but the recent publication of J.M. da Silva Correia's research provides new information about this theme. He identified two drawings (cat. nos. 56, 57) in the collection of the Museu Nacional as being sceneries for the opera *Didone Abbandonata*, which opened the Salvaterra Theater. In 1754, Giovanni Carlo also produced sceneries for the opera *Adriano in Siria* for the Salvaterra Theater.

His second theater was the Royal Opera House (cat. nos. 61–63), or the Tagus Opera as it was called, because one of the facades faced the river. Located in a continuation of the Ribeira Palace on the west side, it was the first great theater built in Portugal. With this construction, Lisbon became part of the network of large European cities with theaters built by the Bibiena family. Giovanni Carlo drew and executed the stage for the operas performed in this beautiful new theater. Etchings that illustrate the librettos of operas performed there were made after his drawings and thus suggest the appearance of the sets. The theater was inaugurated with the opera *Alessandro nell'Indie* on the occasion of Queen Mariana Victoria's birthday. Although her birthday proper was on 31 March 1755, the celebration was postponed to 2 April to avoid conflicting with Lent.

A detailed description of this building has not been found, but its contemporaries described it as "sumptuous" and "magnificent." It opened in early April and was destroyed by an earthquake seven months later on 1 November. Nothing remained of it, since the ruins, depicted with some fantasy in an etching by Jacques Philippe Le Bas (cat. no. 64), were demolished as part of the Lisbon reconstruction plan. The building was set lengthwise along the Tagus, where the Navy Arsenal is now, with its main elevation on the east side near the palace.

In spite of the great shock and the loss of his possessions as a result of the great earthquake of 1755, João Carlos Bibiena (as he was already called locally) wrote to his brother Luigi Antonio in Bologna to say that he was alive and well with the whole family. Writing under the shelter of a tent on 12 November, he mentioned in particular his son, "il mio Giovanni." The family, however, was not exactly the same as before. He had become a widower in Portugal and had married again, this time to a Portuguese woman, on 5 February 1755. Marriage records confirm that his new wife, Rosa Maria de Jesus, was also a widow and the marriage was celebrated in the parish of Santa Catarina do Monte Sinai, but nothing is said about the death of Isabella Beccari.

After the horror and devastation of the catastrophic earthquake, life had to return to normal habits and traditional customs. The king and the court needed new quarters, for the old palace (i.e., the Palace of Conde de Óbidos, in Ajuda) was not large enough. Bibiena was commissioned to construct a temporary palace, which, despite its rather vast size, deserved its picturesque name "Royal Shed" due to the wood, canvas, and brick employed. This residence must have contrasted dramatically with the sturdy stone structure of the collapsed Ribeira Palace. A later drawing in the National Library published by Carvalho gives an idea of the number of rooms and compartments of the new royal house. As Carvalho states, the design and decoration of this project must have given João Carlos Bibiena ample opportunity to use his ingenuity and imagination as a scenographer. Here he built his last theater.

Two Englishmen, Nathaniel Wraxall and Richard Twiss, made descriptions of this theater, which were quoted by later authors and transcribed by Marita McClymonds. The small opera house had a capacity of 130 spectators. Instead of boxes, it contained a raised gallery for the royal family and two apron stage boxes for the Patriarch and high ranking foreigners. Despite its size, it satisfied the court's taste for opera performances.

Another important task, pursued with great zeal by King Joseph, was the construction of the royal chapel adjoining the palace. Built in stone with the interior overlaid in wood, it was no more than the principles of theater design applied to religious architecture. Yet, after all, religious architecture often provided the stage for feasts and theatrical sacred functions. One of the best descriptions of these stagings is reported in a letter written by Bibiena and published by Carvalho. João Carlos noted with a certain pride the performance he planned for the celebration of a solemn *Te Deum* in the chapel of Sta. Maria da Ajuda, in thanks for the king's safe escape from an assassination attempt. The novelty of the performance came, according to Bibiena, from the Bolognese taste, which he introduced in this type of representation.

He continued to divide his activity between architecture and scenography in and out of the theater. In September 1760, the king appointed him supernumerary architect of the royal palaces and manors. In the same year João Carlos started work on the church of N. Sra. do Livramento or Memória. The first stone was laid on 3 September, but this structure was in the end built by the architect Mateus Vicente, because on 3 October 1760, at the age of forty-three, Giovanni Carlo Sicinio Galli Bibiena died in the parish of Ajuda, where he lived. His name had changed to João Carlos Bibiena because not long before he had become a Portuguese citizen, like so many other Italians who lived there.

Similar to Bibiena, other Italian artists, including Petronio Mazonni and Giacomo Azzolini, journeyed to Portugal to work in scenography and to perform as musicians, singers, or dancers. Standing out among the Portuguese who continued in theatrical work is Inácio de Oliveira Bernardes. Yet the truth is neither Bibiena's companions nor his followers possessed his artistic personality. Like other members of his family, João Carlos combined theoretical knowledge and technical professionalism with a creative imagination and enthusiastic fantasy. His presence in Lisbon, particularly when King Joseph exercised such a keen interest in opera, was crucial to the exceptional importance of those years in the history of Portuguese theater.

Even though few drawings can be safely attributed to João Carlos, a refinement and evolution in taste are evident when these drawings are compared with those by his father. Francesco's drawings exude a vigorous, vibrant, decorative thrill that is framed by the agitated architecture of his sceneries (cat. nos. 16–20). Works by João Carlos are discreetly permeated by a more rational balance with a neo-classical touch, as in the sceneries for *L'Olimpiade* (cat. no. 60). Moreover, he utilized various traditional formulas in his freely created drawings and etchings for the sceneries.

For viewers, however, the most exciting aspect of this exhibition is imagining being in the Royal Opera House and attending one of these extraordinary performances of sound and vision.

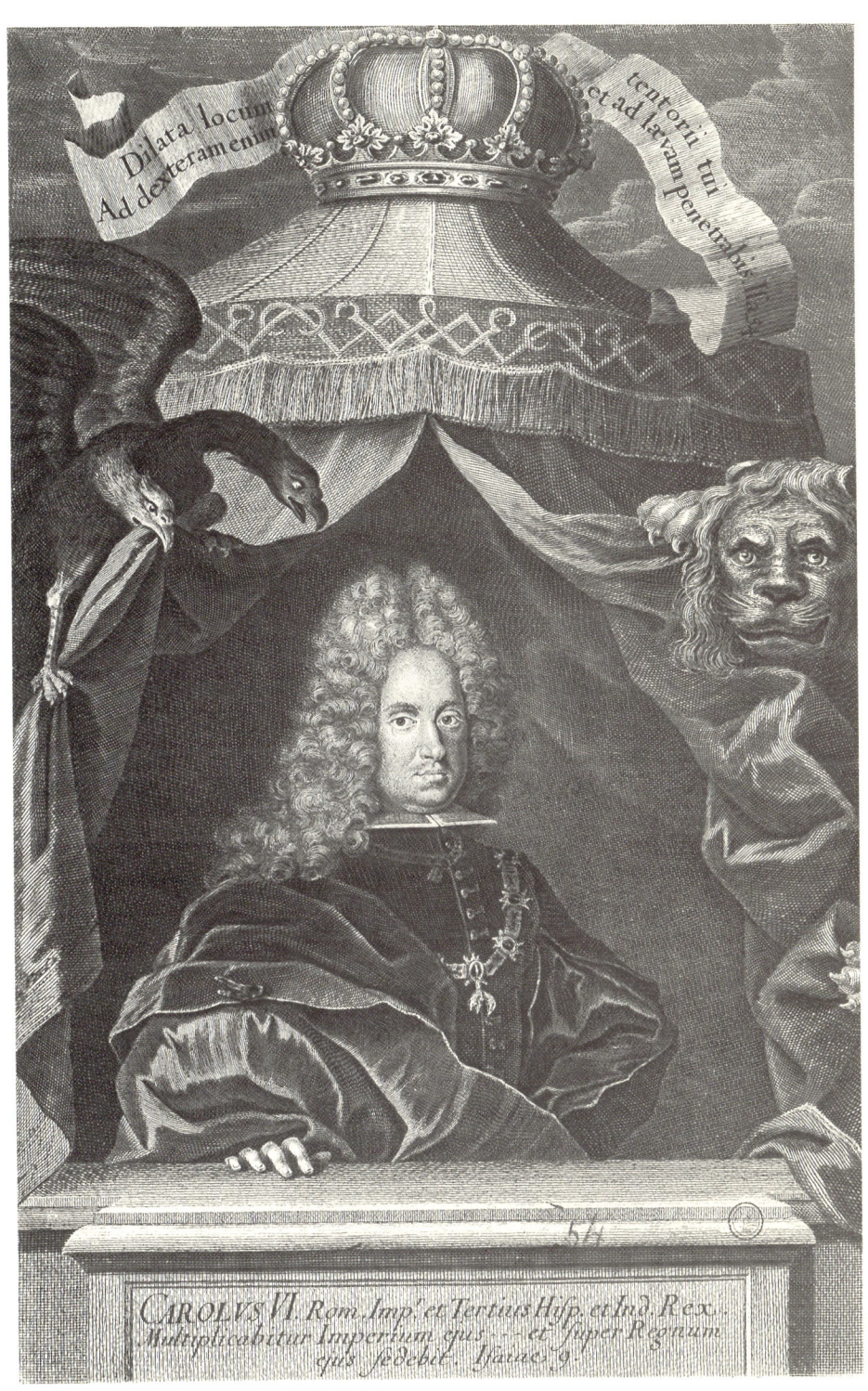

1. Martin Bernigerotti, *Portrait of Charles VI*, etching

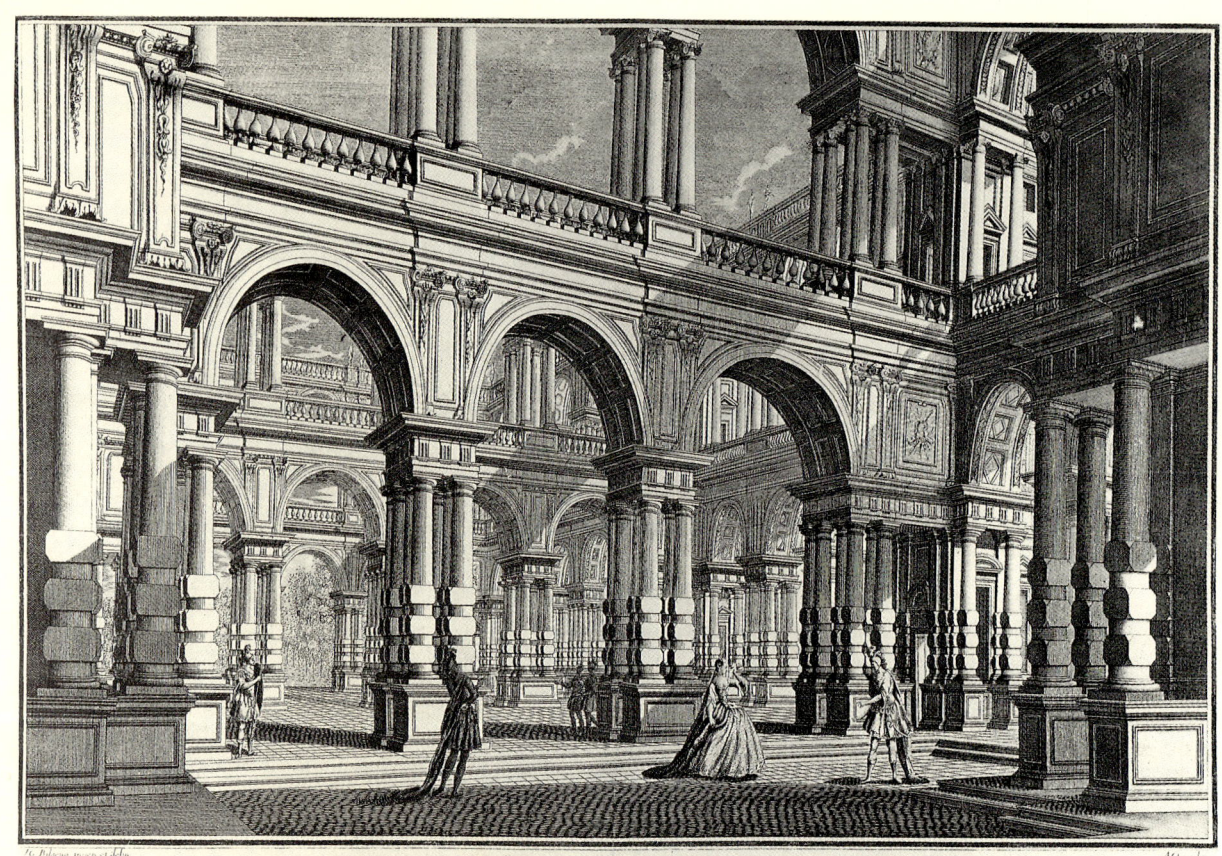

2. Giuseppe Bibiena, *Study for a Stage Set*, etching

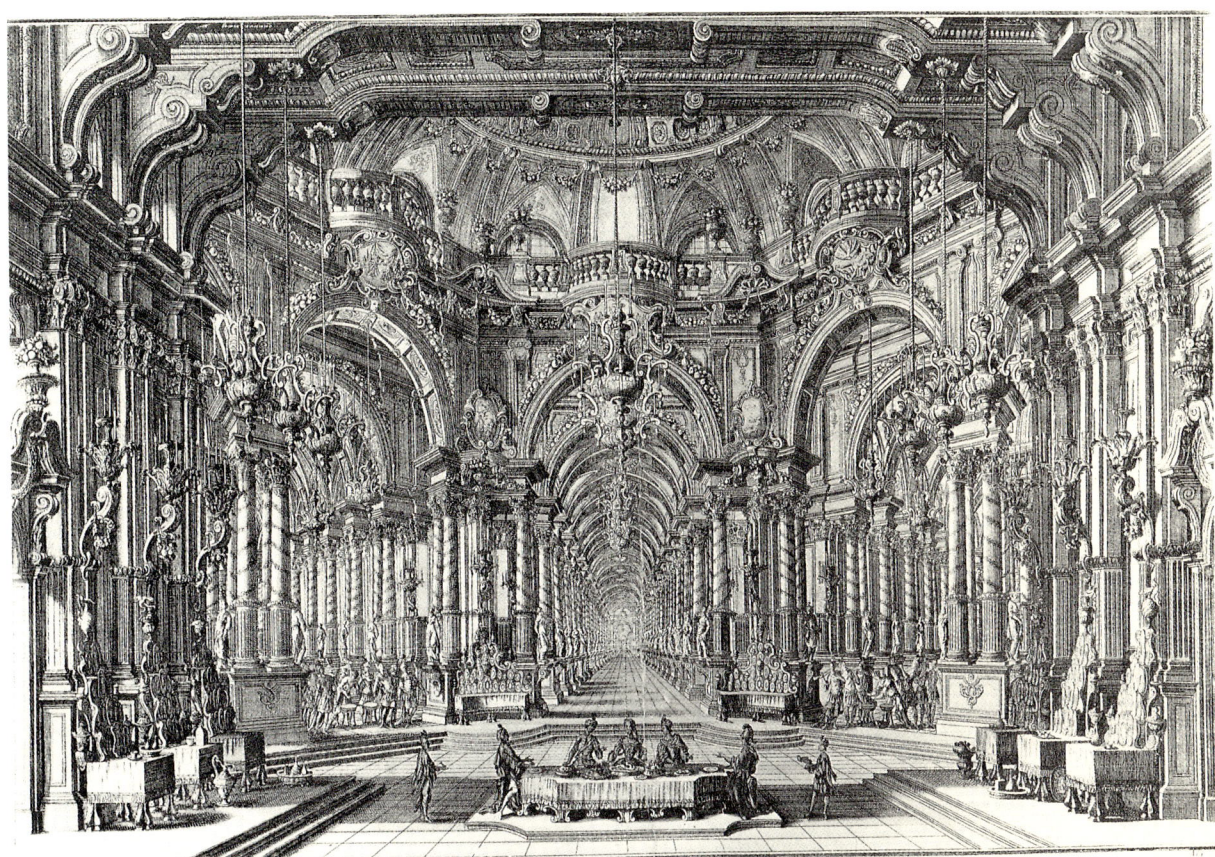

3. Giuseppe Bibiena, *Study for a Stage Set*, etching

22

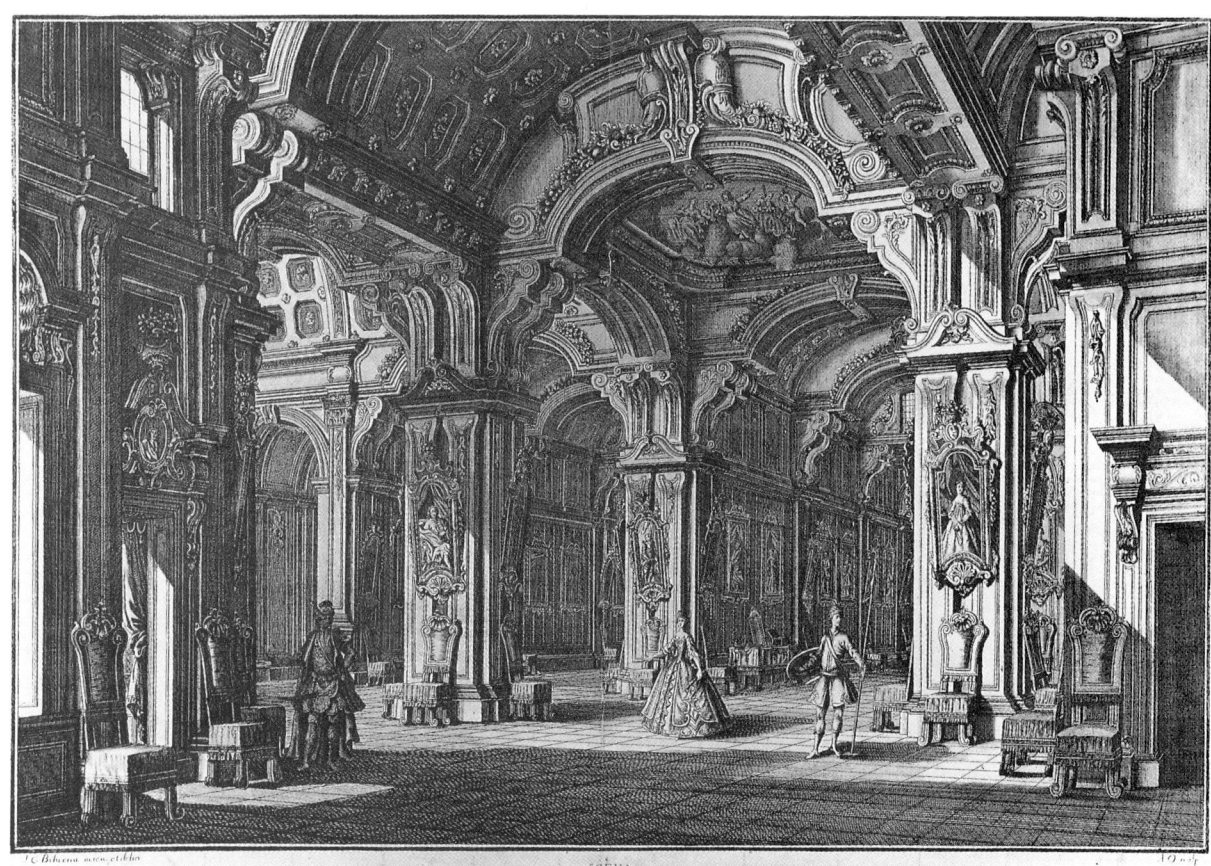

4. Giuseppe Bibiena, *Study for a Stage Set*, etching

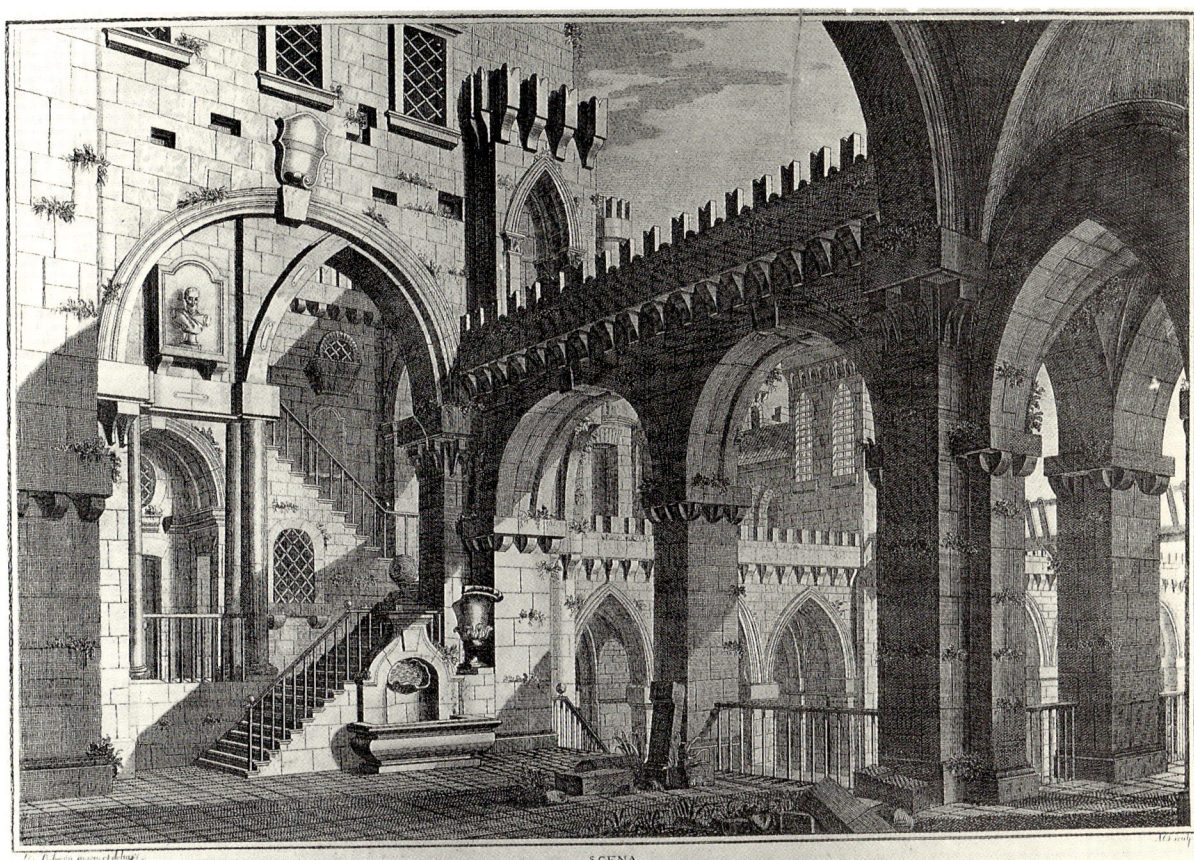

5. Giuseppe Bibiena, *Study for a Stage Set*, etching

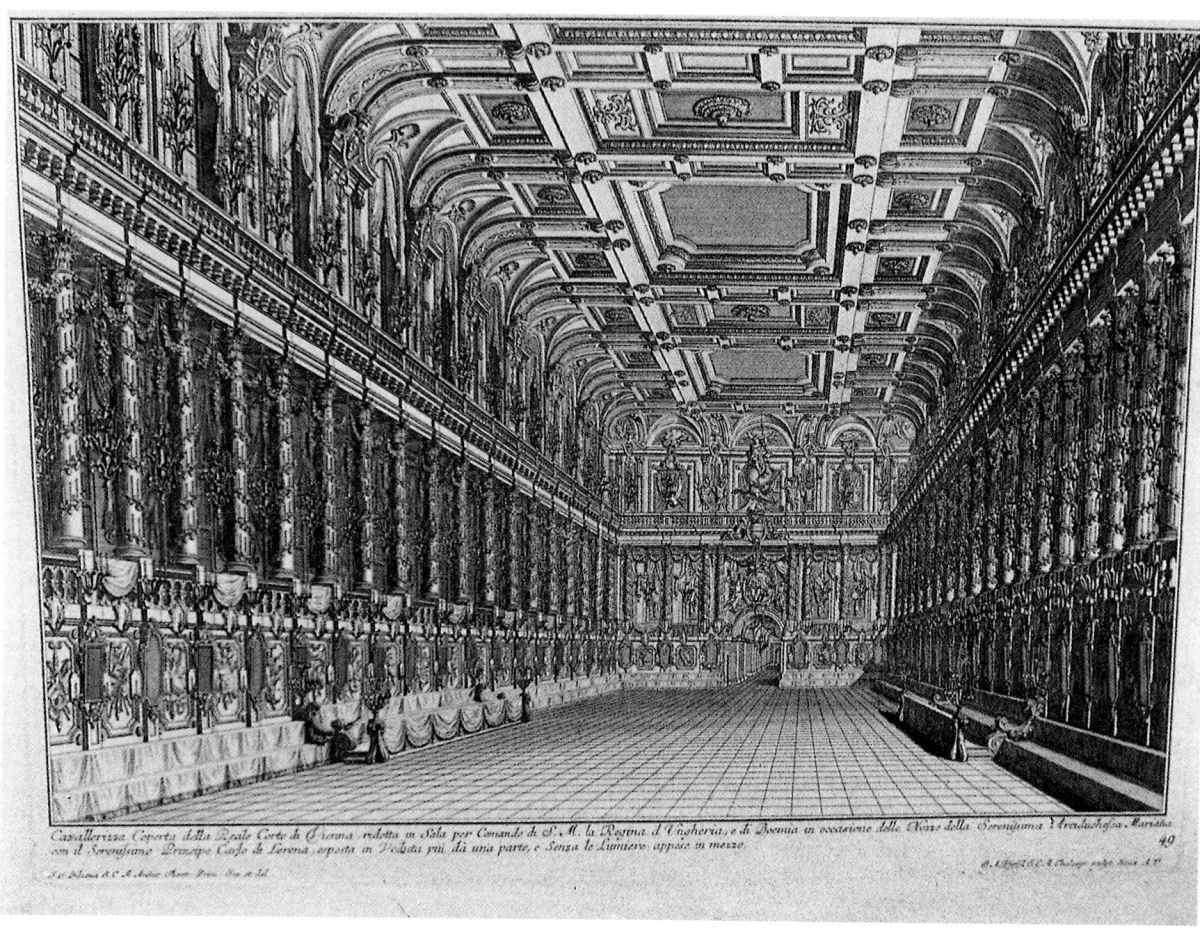

6. Giuseppe Bibiena, *Riding School Converted into a Grand Hall*, etching

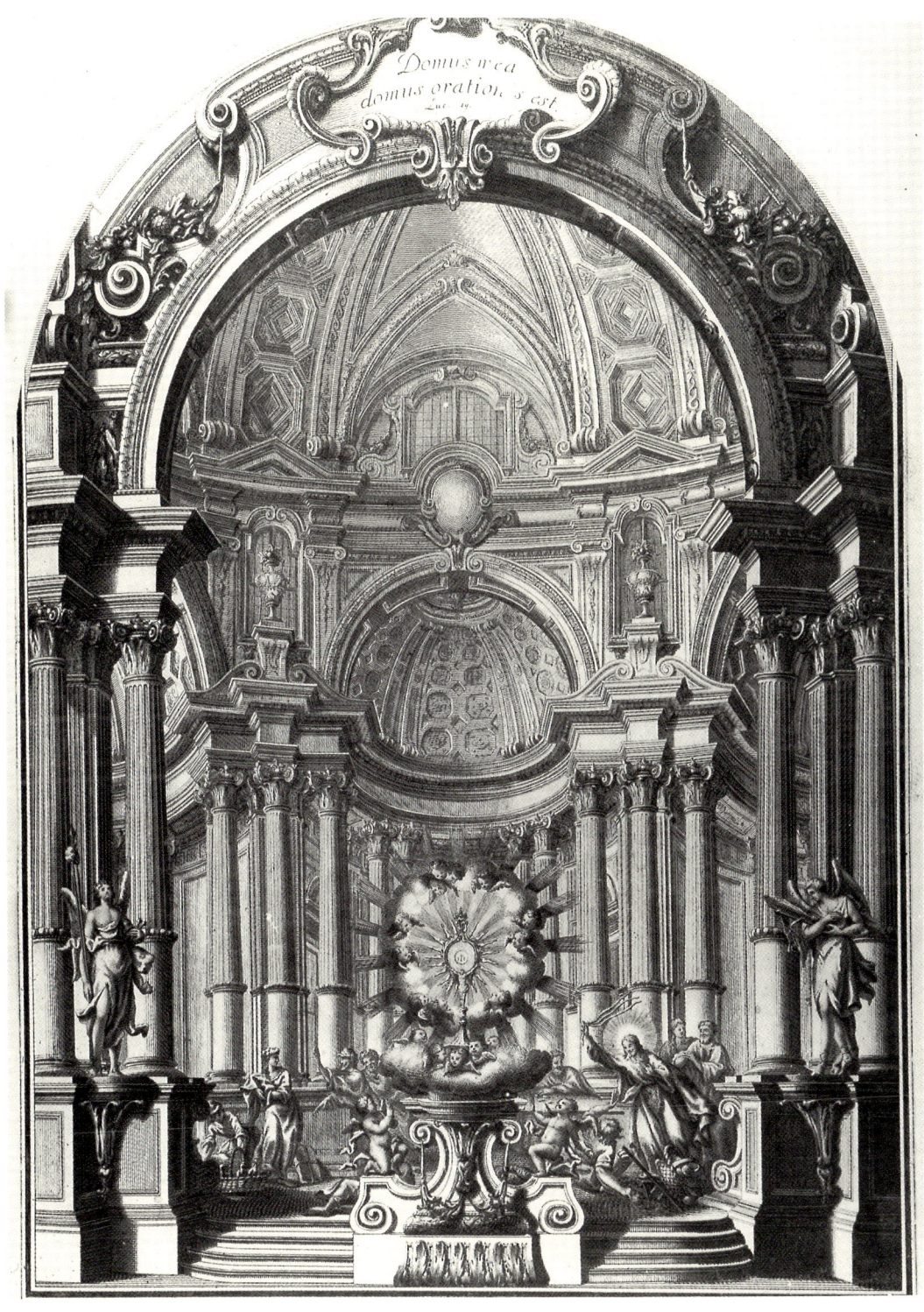

7. Lorenzo Zucchi, *Architectural Study: "Expulsion of the Peddlers from the Temple,"* etching

L'ARCHITETTURA CIVILE
PREPARATA SÙ LA GEOMETRIA,
E RIDOTTA ALLE PROSPETTIVE.
CONSIDERAZIONI PRATICHE
DI
FERDINANDO GALLI BIBIENA
CITTADINO BOLOGNESE

ARCHITETTO PRIMARIO, CAPO MASTRO MAGGIORE, E PITTORE
DI CAMERA, E FESTE DI TEATRO DELLA MAESTA'
DI CARLO III. IL MONARCA DELLE SPAGNE

DISSEGNATE, E DESCRITTE IN CINQUE PARTI.

La prima contiene la Geometria, e avvertimenti, prima che à fabbricar si pervenga.

La seconda. Un Trattato dell'Architettura civile in generale, e le divisioni di essa molto facilitate.

La Terza. La Prospettiva commune, orizontale, e di sotto in sù.

La Quarta. Un brieve discorso di Pittura, e la Prospettiva per li Pittori di Figure, colla nuova Prospettiva delle Scene Teatrali vedute per angolo, oltre le praticate da tutti gli altri.

La Quinta. La Mecanica, ò arte di movere, reggere, e trasportar pesi.

DEDICATA
Alla Sacra Cattolica Real Maestà
DI CARLO III.
RE DELLE SPAGNE, D'UNGHERIA, BOEMIA &c.

IN PARMA,
Per Paolo Monti MCDCCXI.
CON LICENZA DE' SUPERIORI.

8. Ferdinando Bibiena, *Civil Architecture Composed with Respect to Geometry and Reduced to the Perspective and Practical Consideration of Ferdinando Galli Bibiena . . .* , book

DIREZIONI

A' Giovani Studenti nel Disegno dell' Architettura Civile,

NELL' ACCADEMIA CLEMENTINA

Dell' Instituto delle Scienze,

UNITE

DA FERDINANDO GALLI BIBIENA

Cittadino Bolognese, Accademico Clementino, Architetto primario, e Pittore di Camera, e feste Teatrali

DI S. M. CES., E CAT.

Divise in cinque parti

TOMO PRIMO

Con nuova aggiunta

DEDICATE DALL' AUTORE

A S. CATTARINA

DE VIGRI DA BOLOGNA

Protettrice della suddetta Accademia

Seconda Edizione.

IN BOLOGNA

Nella Stamperìa di Lelio dalla Volpe. 1745.

Con licenza de' Superiori.

9. Ferdinando Bibiena, *Guide to Young Students in the Design of Civil Architecture at the Accademia Clementina of the Institute of Science. . . .*, book

1346
DIREZIONI
Della Prospettiva Teorica
Corrispondenti a quelle dell'Architettura
ISTRUZIONE
A' Giovani Studenti di Pittura, e Architettura
NELL' ACCADEMIA CLEMENTINA
Dell' Instituto delle Scienze,
RACCOLTE
DA FERDINANDO GALLI BIBIENA
Cittadino Bolognese, Accademico Clementino, Architetto primario, e Pittore
di Camera, e feste Teatrali
DI S. M. CES., E CAT.
Divise in cinque parti
TOMO SECONDO
DEDICATE DALL' AUTORE
A S. PETRONIO
Vescovo, e principal Protettore
di Bologna.
Seconda Edizione.

IN BOLOGNA

Nella Stamperìa di Lelio dalla Volpe. 1753.
Con licenza de' Superiori.

10. Ferdinando Bibiena, *Guide to Young Students in the Design of Civil Architecture at the Accademia Clementina of the Institute of Science. . . .*, book

PIANTA, E SPACCATO
DEL NUOVO
TEATRO
DI BOLOGNA.

AL NOBIL UOMO,
ED ECCELSO SIG. SENATORE CO:
GIROLAMO LEGNANI FERRI
GONFALONIERE DI GIUSTIZIA, AMIRAGLIO DELLA
TORRE DI MAGNAVACCA ec. ec. ec.
DA LORENZO CAPPONI.

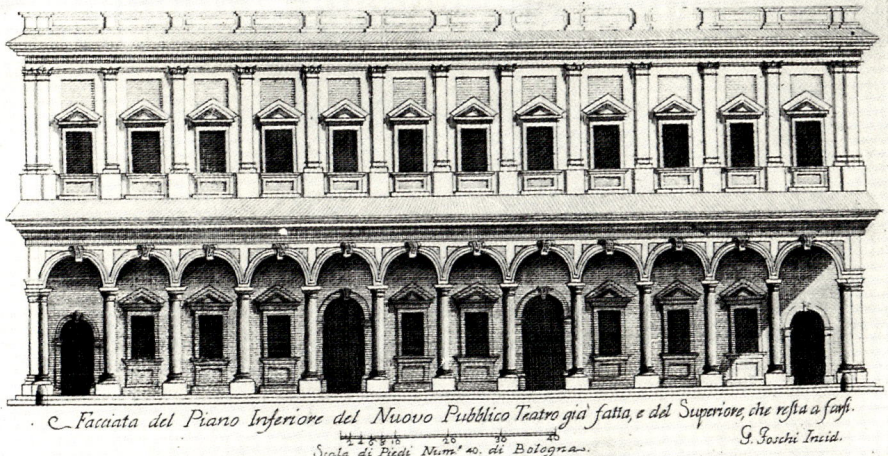

Facciata del Piano Inferiore del Nuovo Pubblico Teatro già fatta, e del Superiore, che resta a farsi.
Scala di Piedi Num.° 40. di Bologna.
G. Foschi Incid.

VENEZIA MDCCLXIV.

11. Lorenzo Capponi, *Plans and Analysis of the New Theater of Bologna. . . .*, book

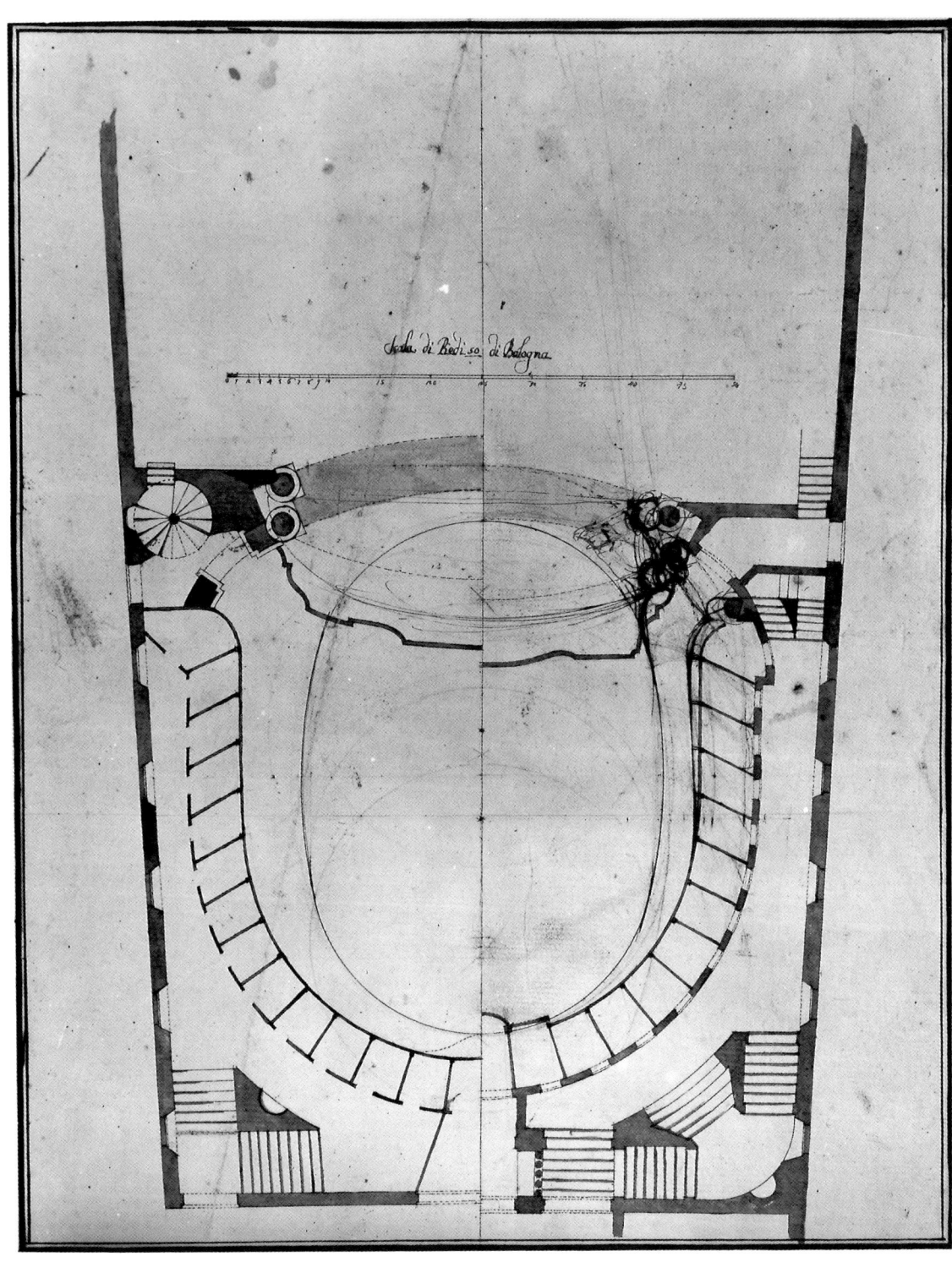

12. António Bibiena, *Plans for a Theater in Bologna*, pen and ink with gray wash

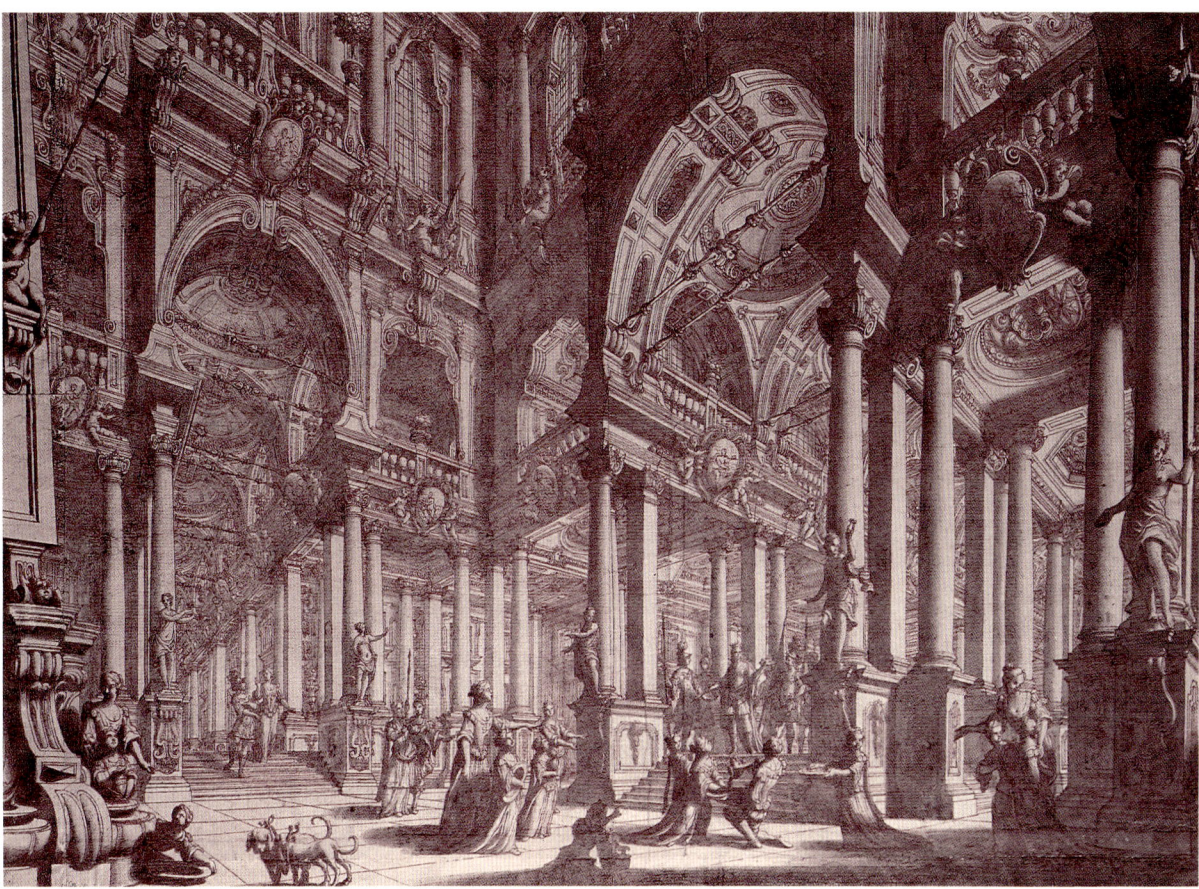

13. Francesco Bibiena, *Grand Atrium with Figures*, pen and ink bistre with sepia and green wash

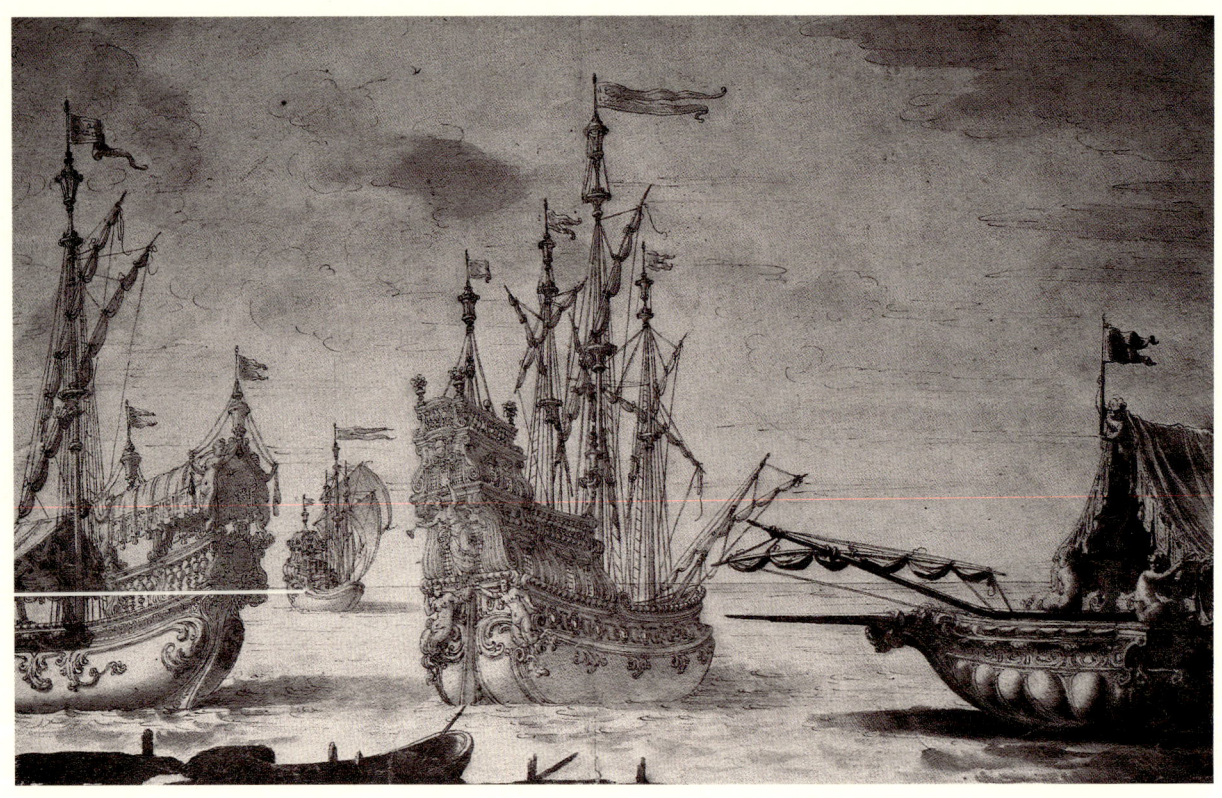

14. Francesco Bibiena, *Stage Scenery with Boats*, pen and ink with sepia wash

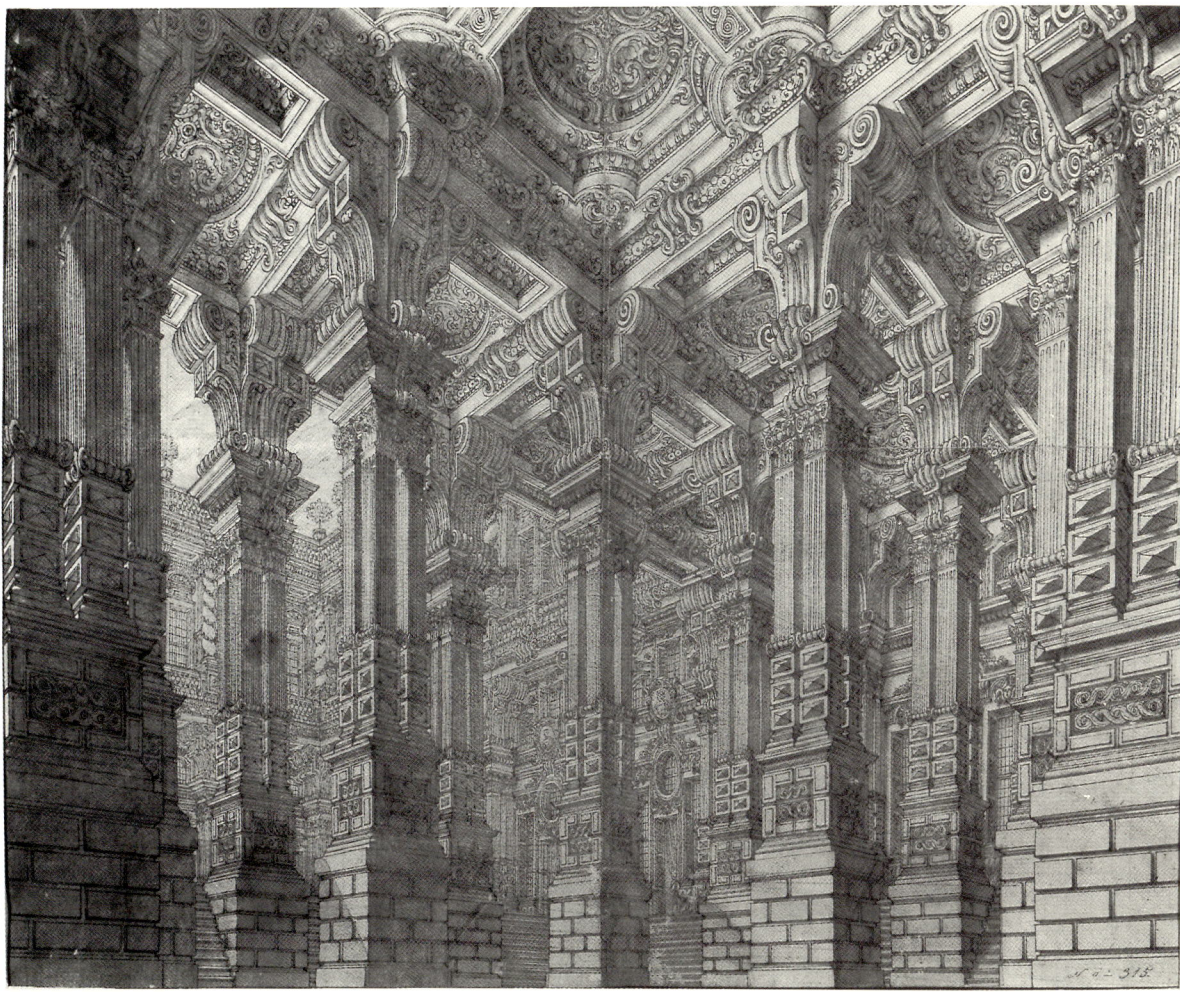

15. Francesco Bibiena, *Grand Atrium*, pen and ink bistre with sepia wash

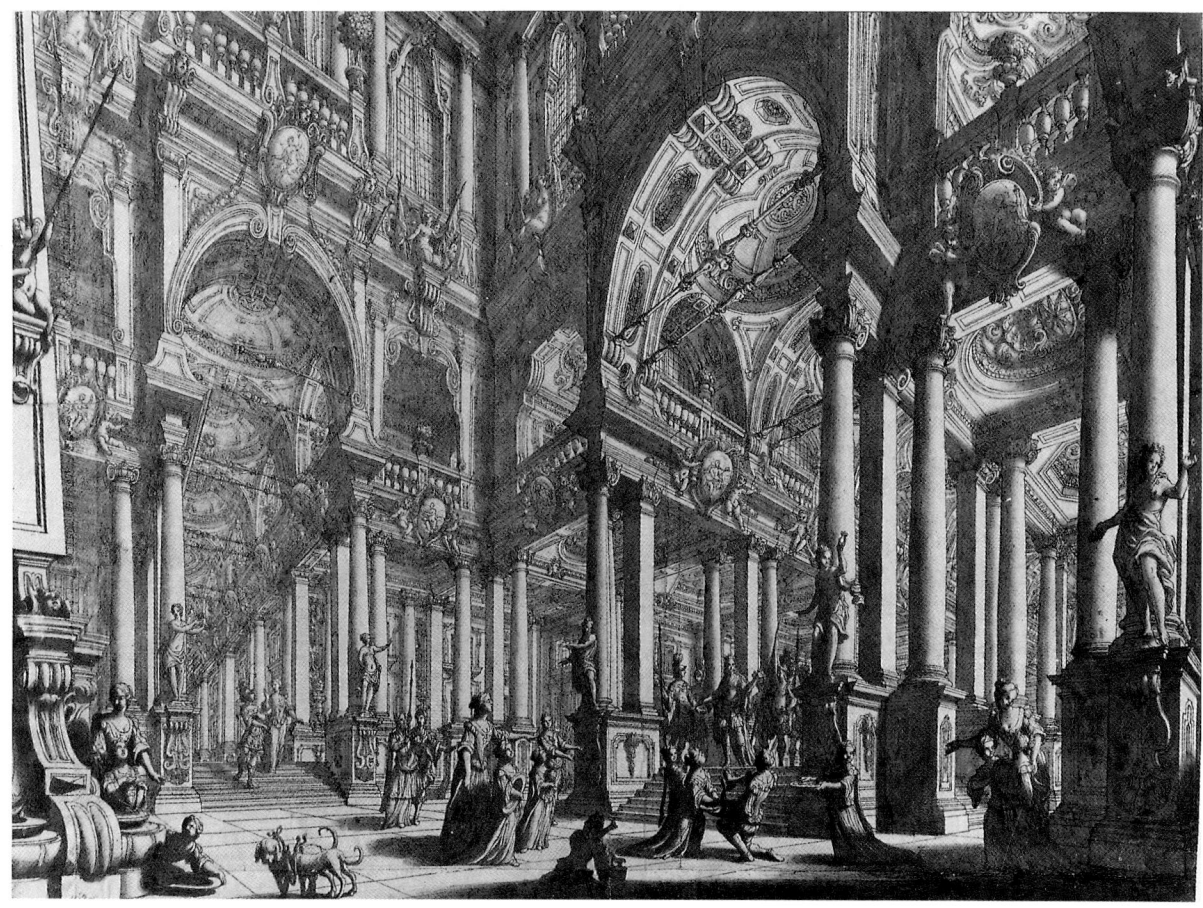

16. Francesco Bibiena, *Interior of a Palace with Staircases*, pen and ink bistre with sepia wash

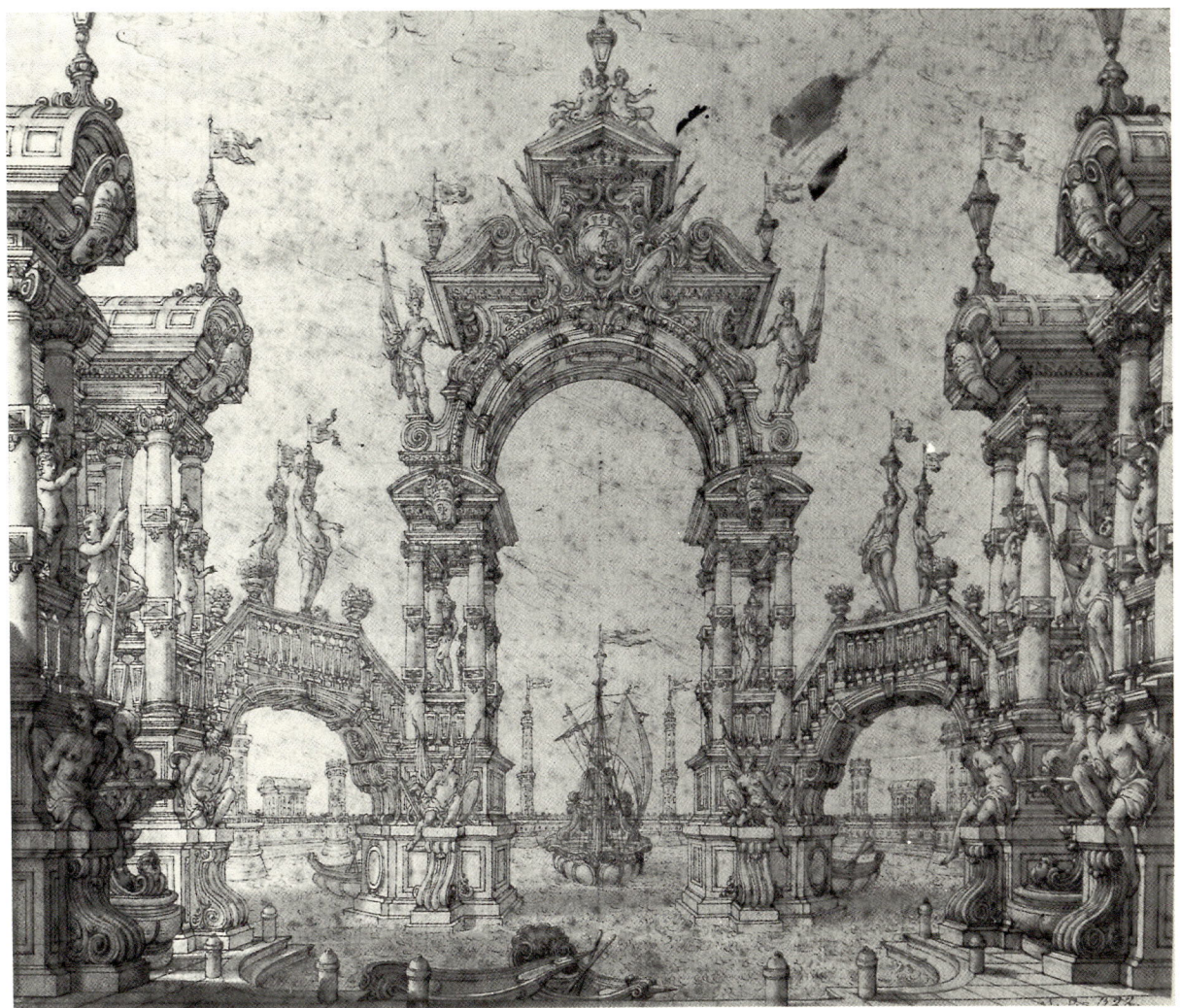

17. Francesco Bibiena, *Grand Harbor with a Triumphal Arch*, pen and ink bistre with sepia wash

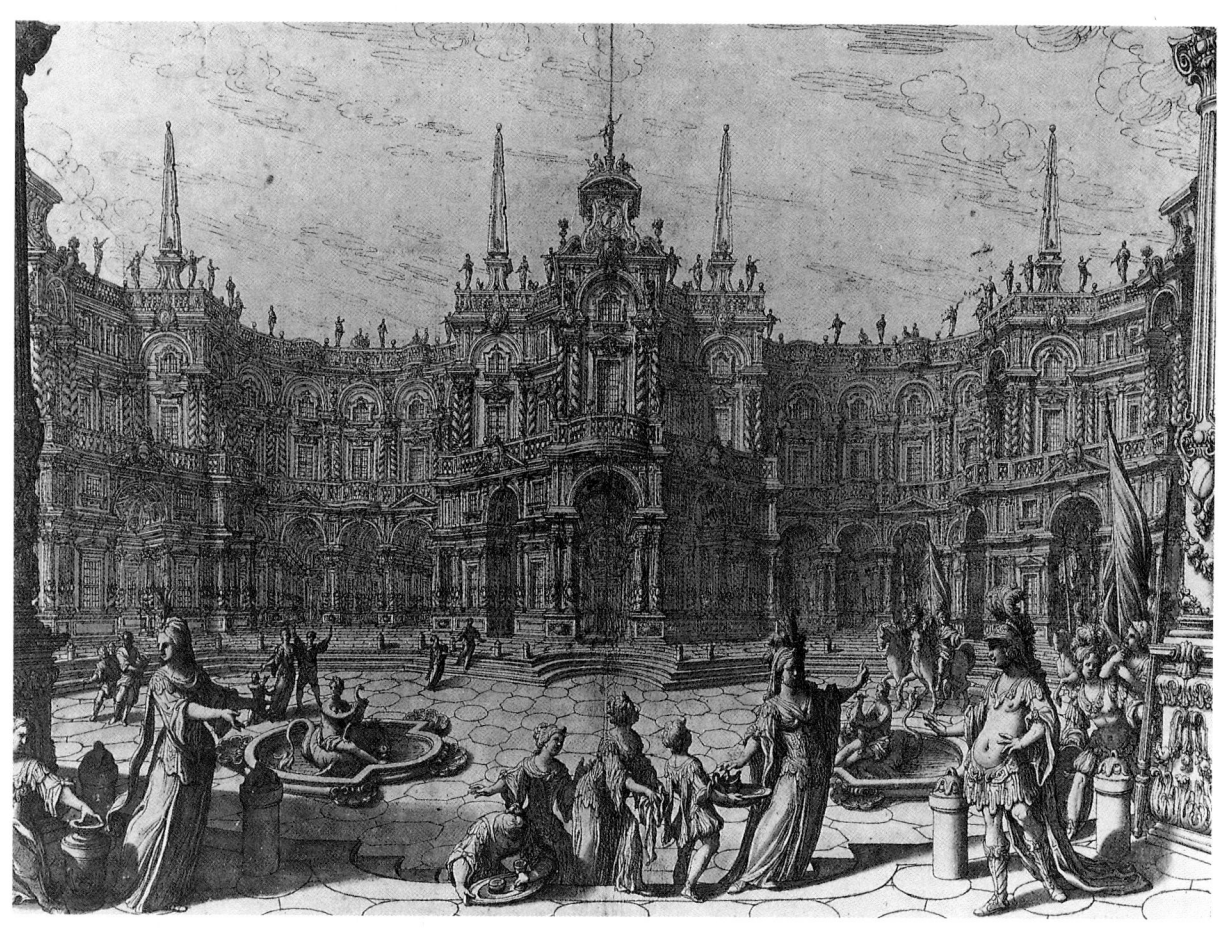

18. Francesco Bibiena, *Grand Courtyard with Figures in the Background*, pen and ink bistre with sepia wash

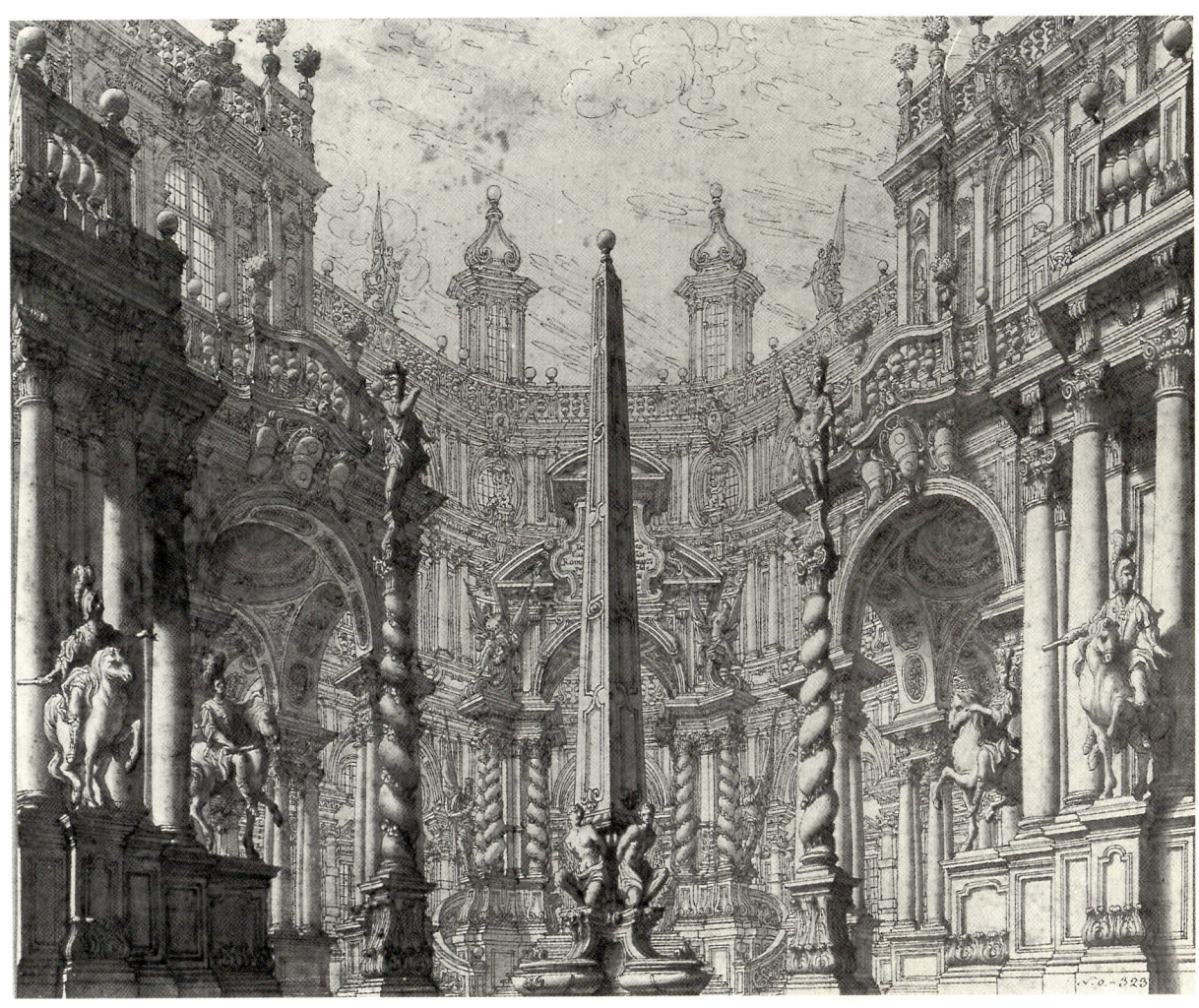

19. Francesco Bibiena, *Structures with an Obelisk as the Focal Point*, pen and ink bistre with sepia wash

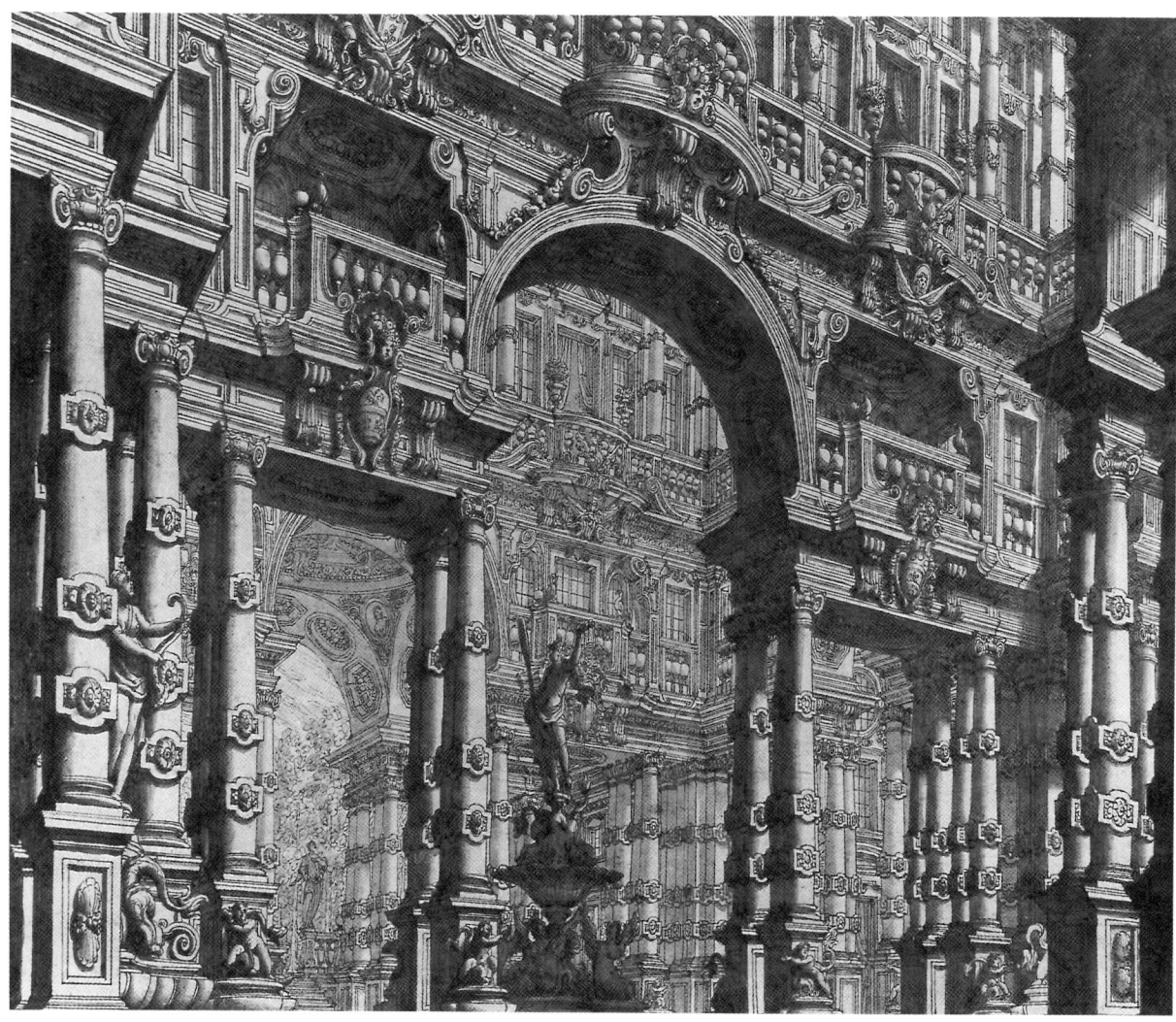

20. Francesco Bibiena, *Arcade of a Courtyard with a Statue of Neptune*, pen and ink bistre with sepia wash

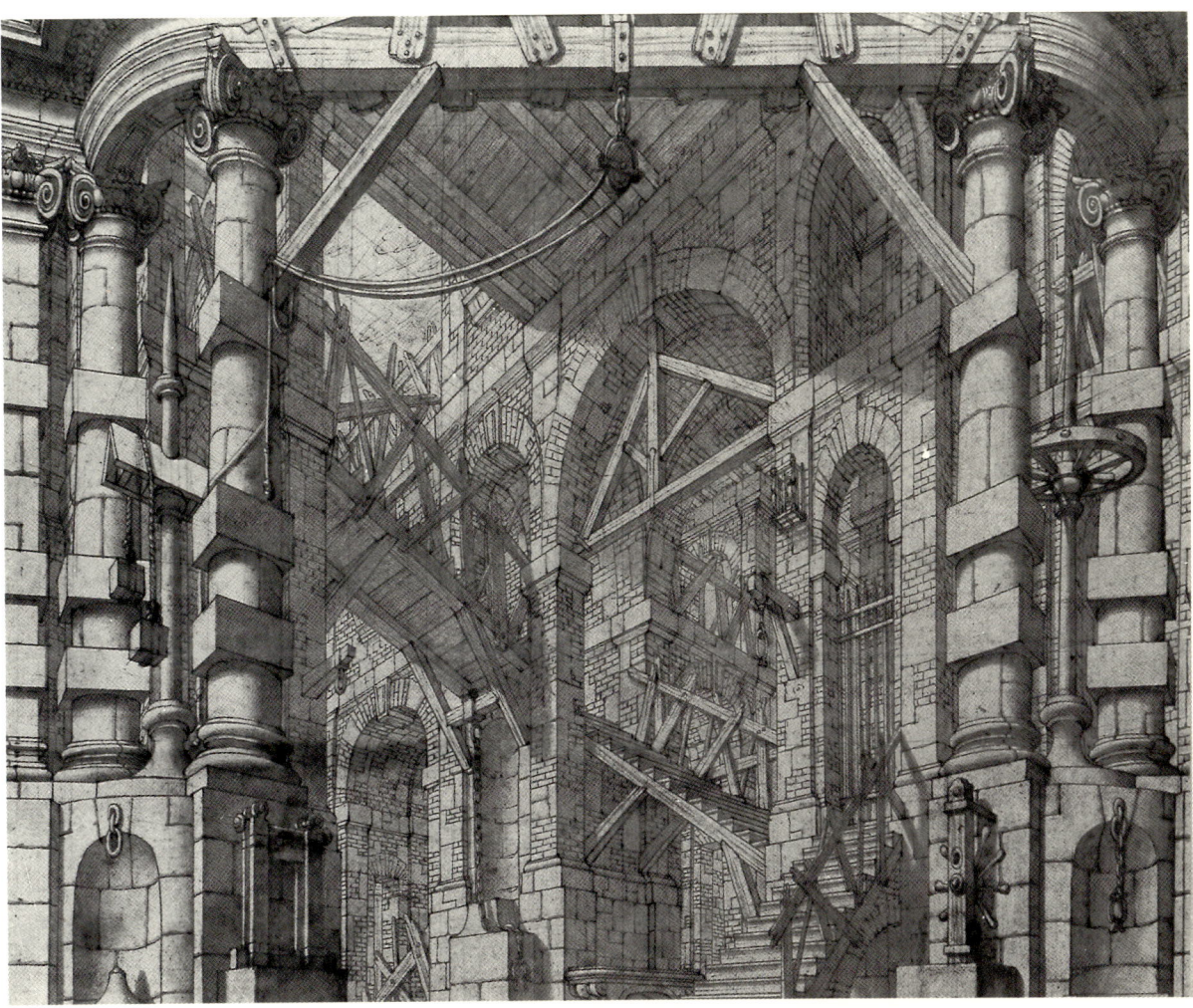

21. Francesco Bibiena, *Prison*, pen and ink with sepia wash

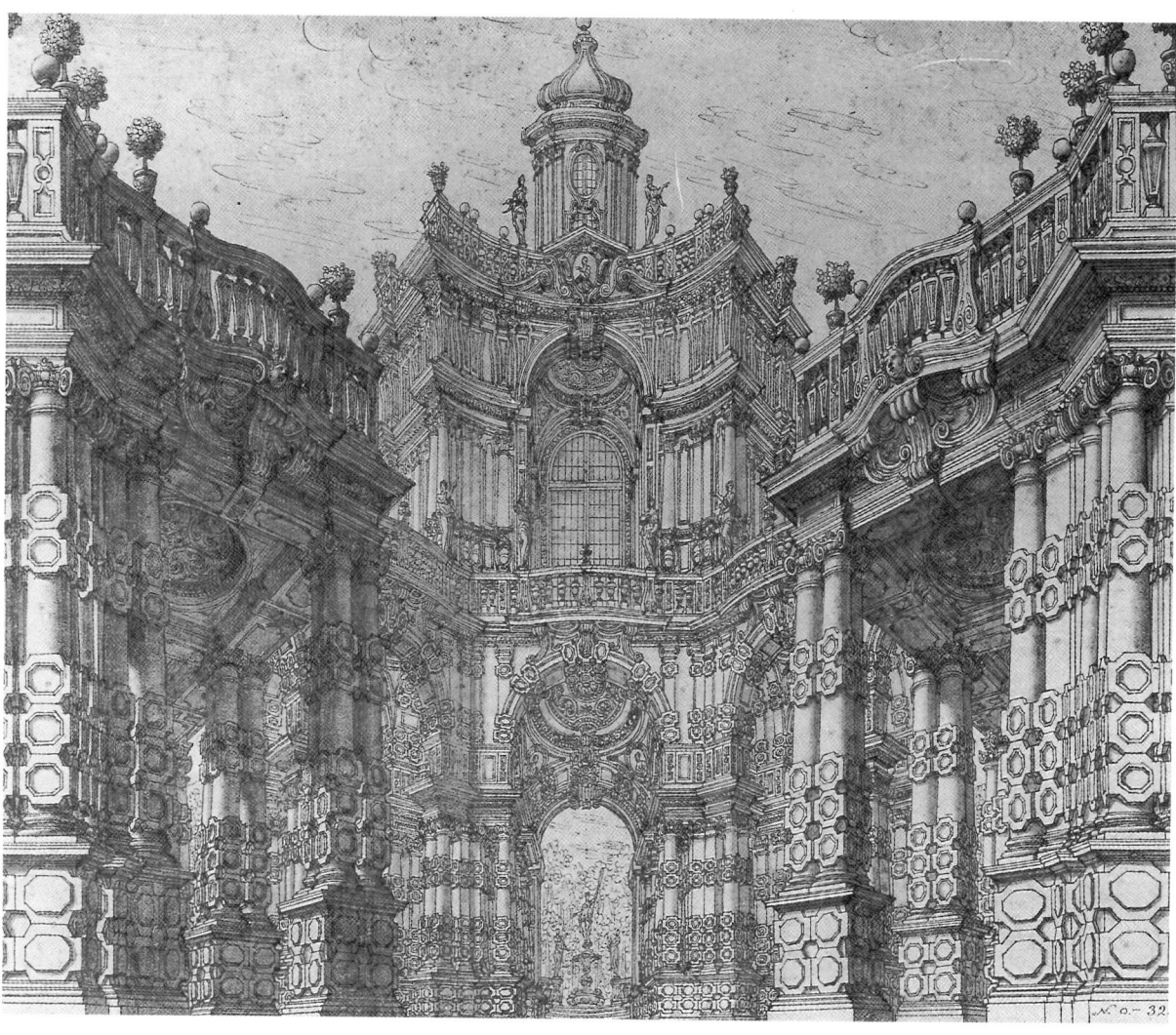

22. Francesco Bibiena, *Grand Loggia Opening onto a Garden*, pen and ink bistre with sepia wash

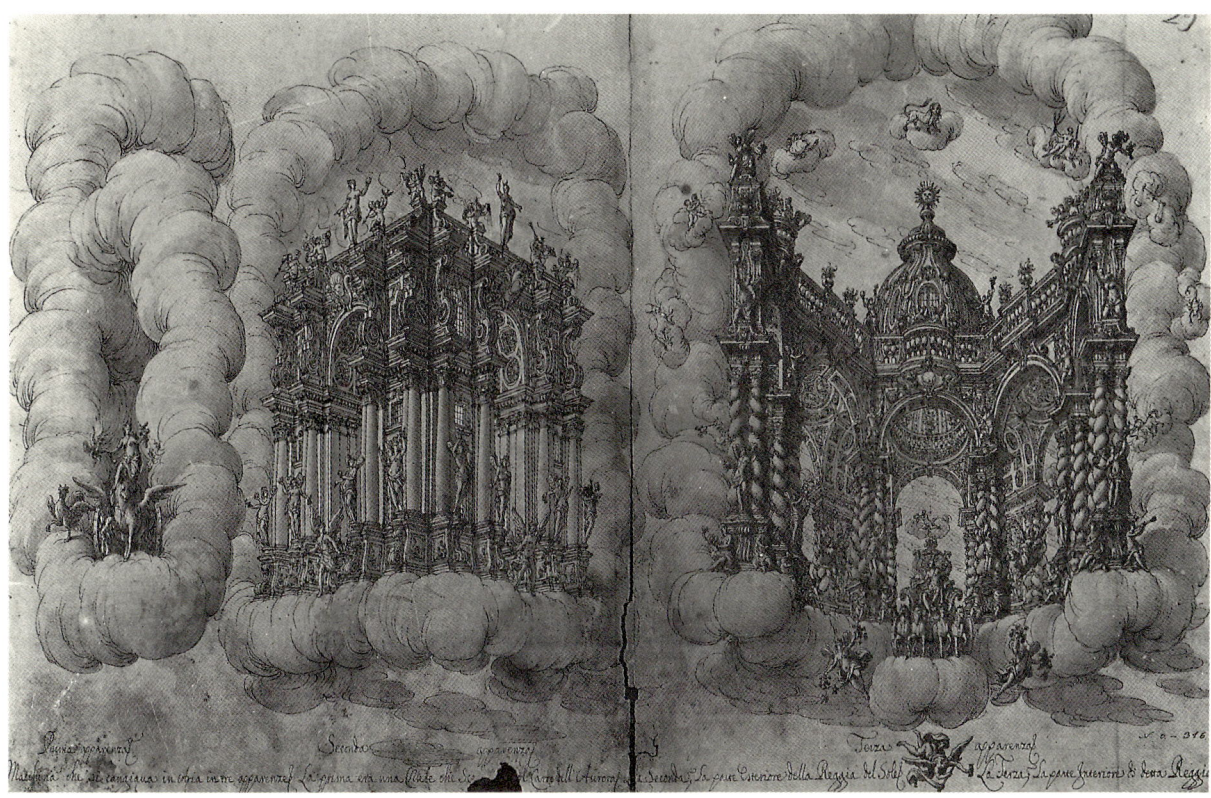

23. Francesco Bibiena, *Theatrical Machines Used for Dance 3, Act 2, Scene 2*, pen and ink with sepia wash

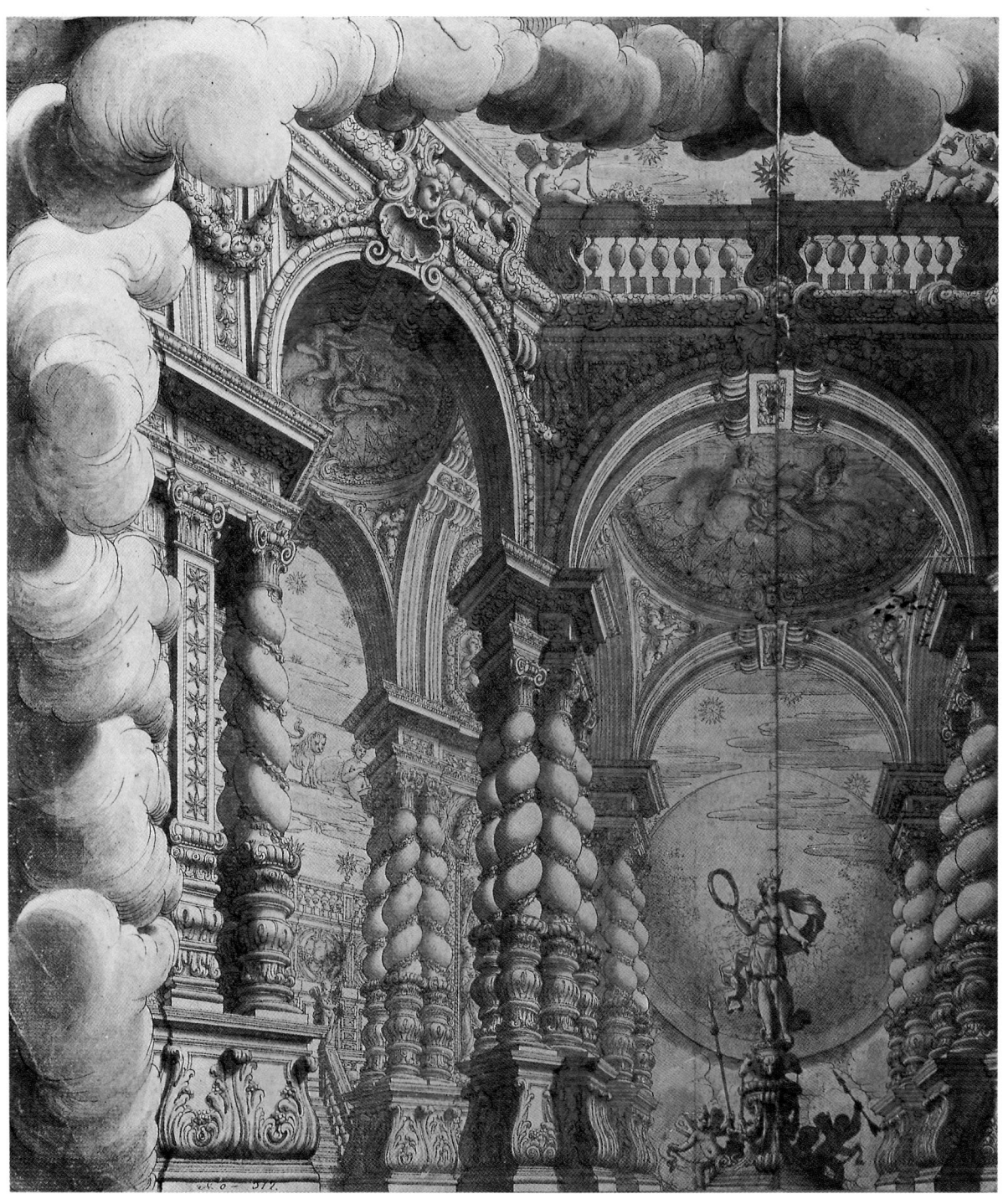

24. Francesco Bibiena, *Atrium of "Royal Palace of the Sun"* or *"The Palace of Diana," Act 3, Scene 9*, pen and ink with sepia wash

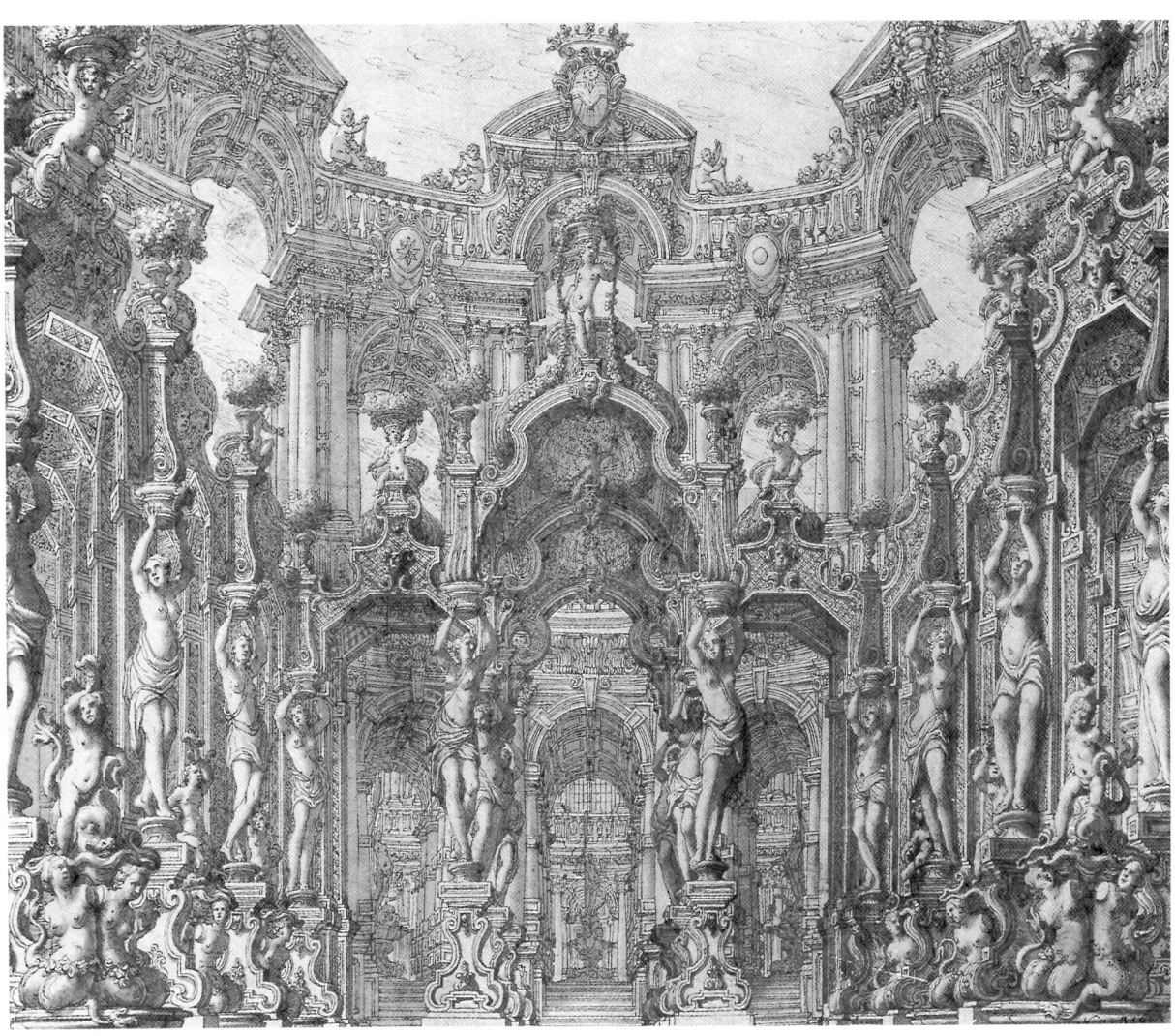

25. Francesco Bibiena, *"Enchanting Royal Palace of Thetis,"*
Act 1, Scene 2, pen and ink bistre with sepia wash

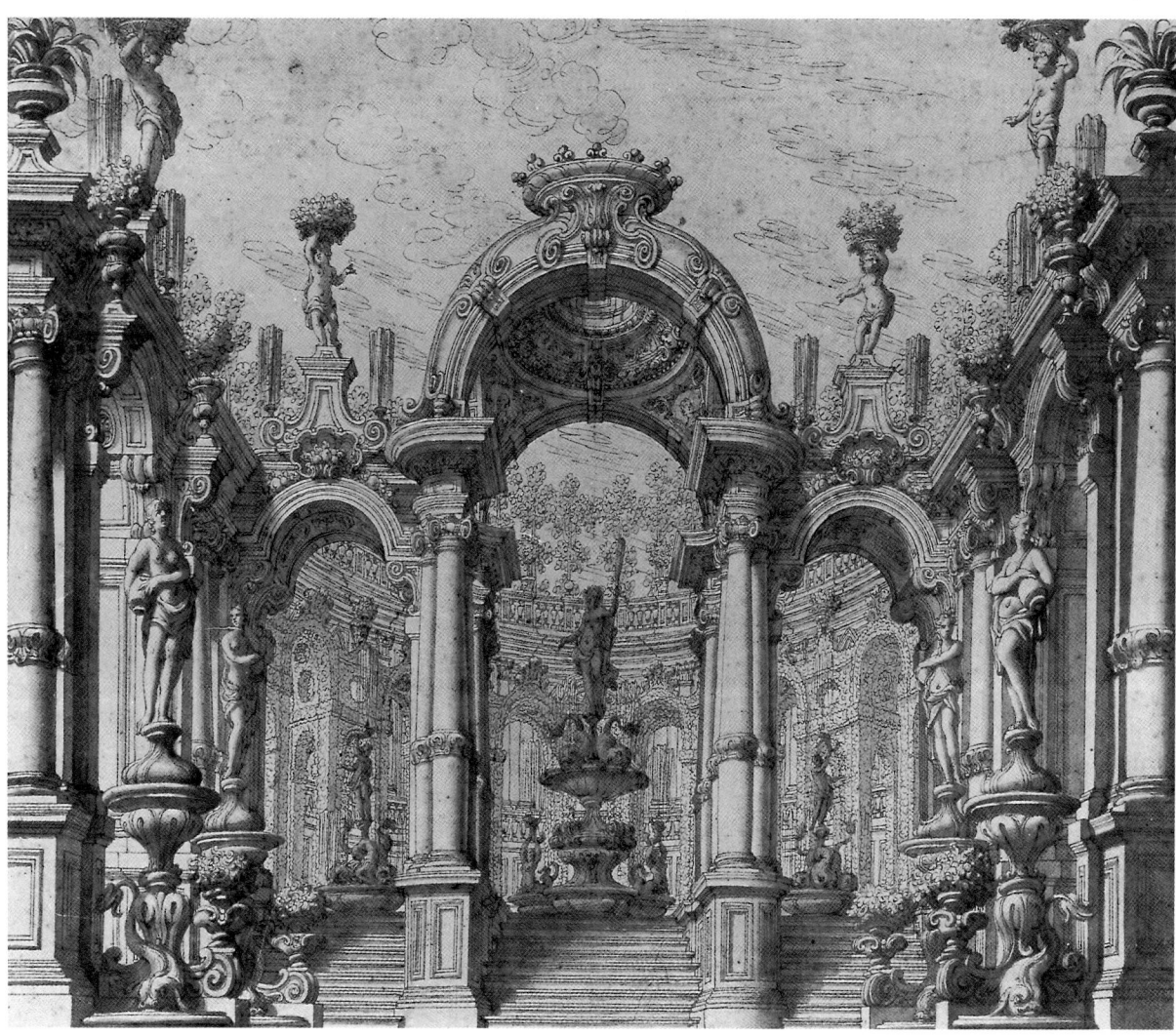

26. Francesco Bibiena, *"Enchanting Royal Palace of Thetis," Pavilion with Fountain*, pen and ink bistre with sepia wash

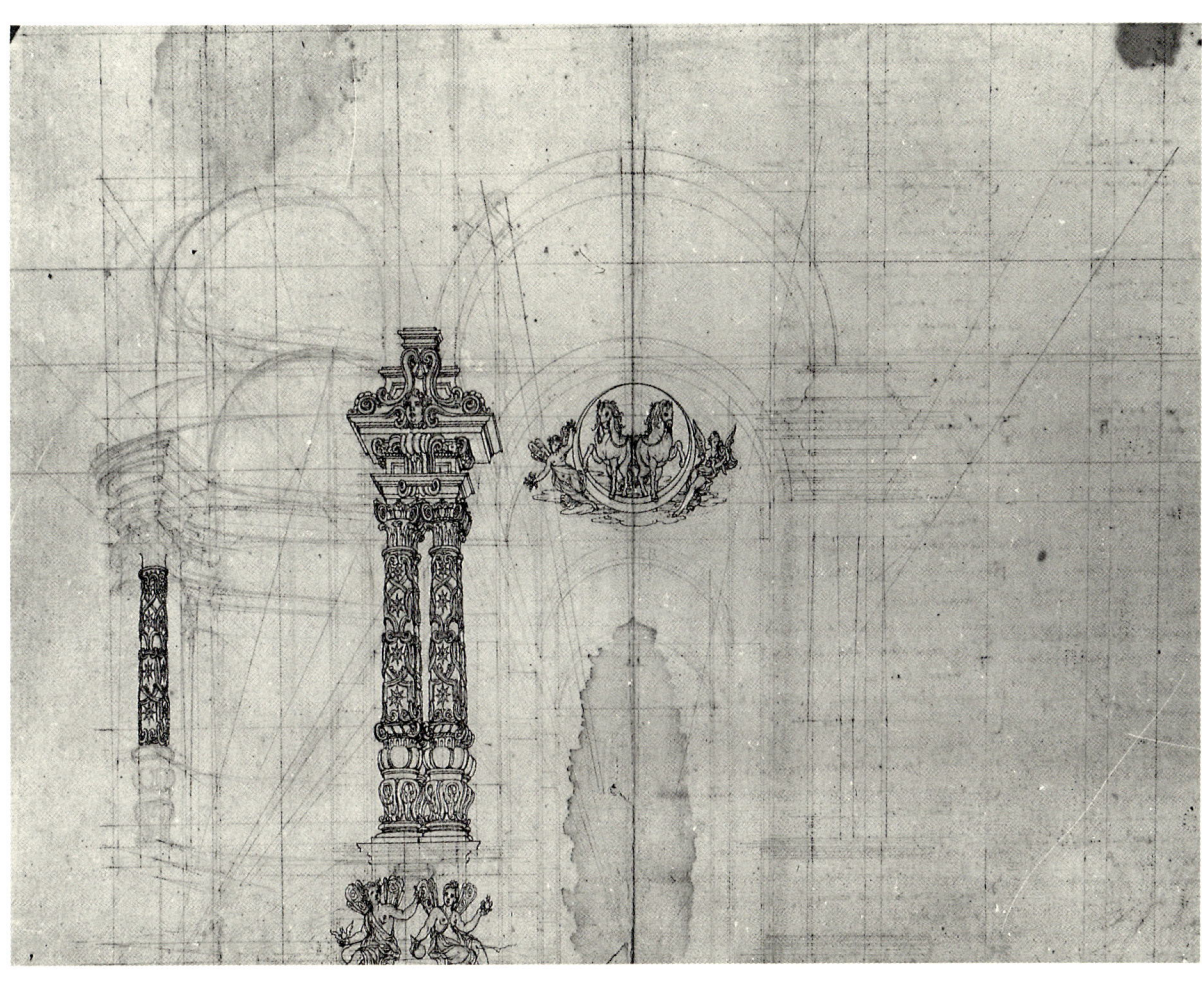

27. Francesco Bibiena, *"Royal Palace of Diana: Symbols of the Hours," Dance 2, Act 2*, pen and ink bistre with sepia wash

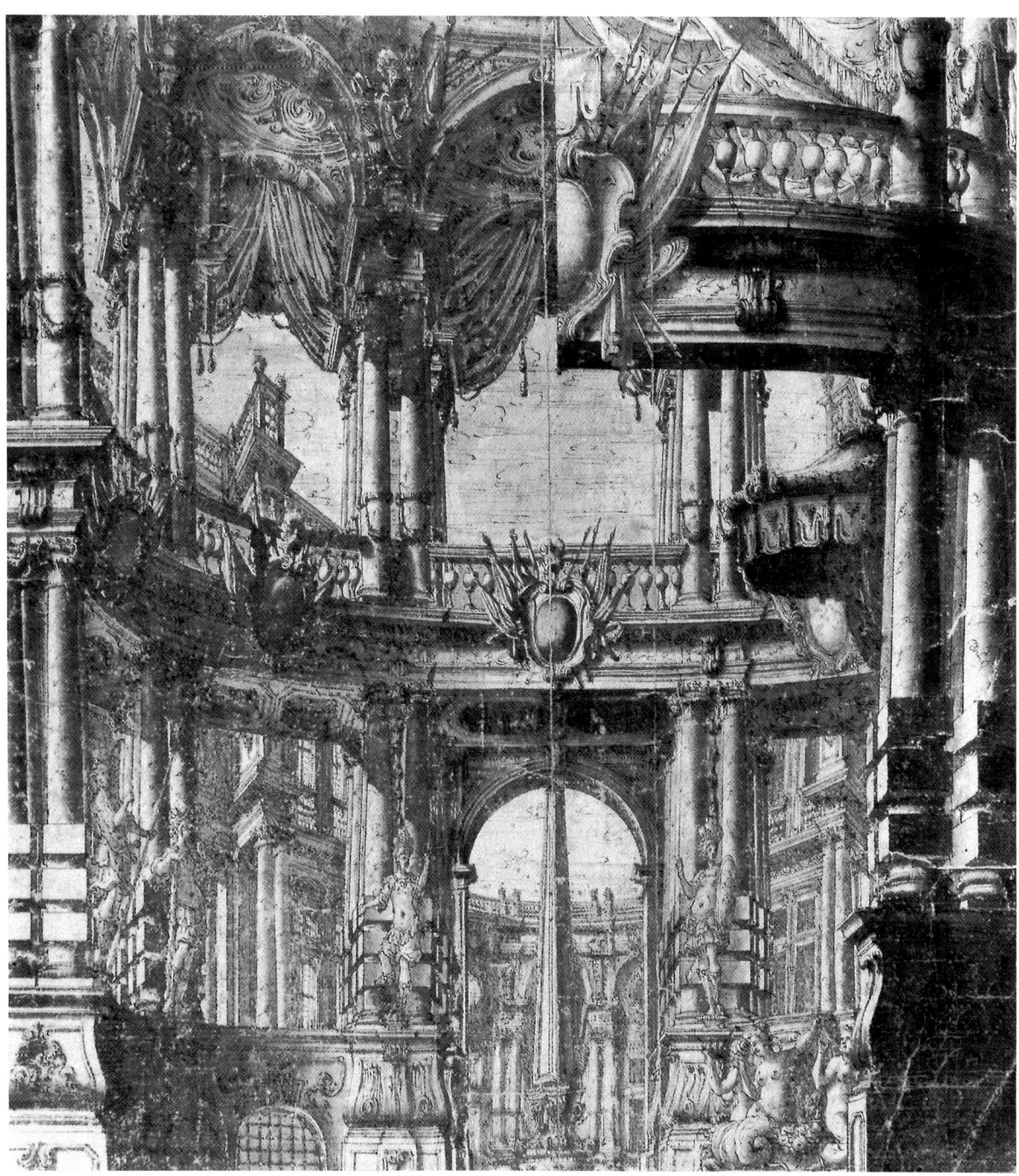

28. Francesco Bibiena, *Amphitheater Scenery with Ostentatious Decoration*, pen and ink with sepia wash

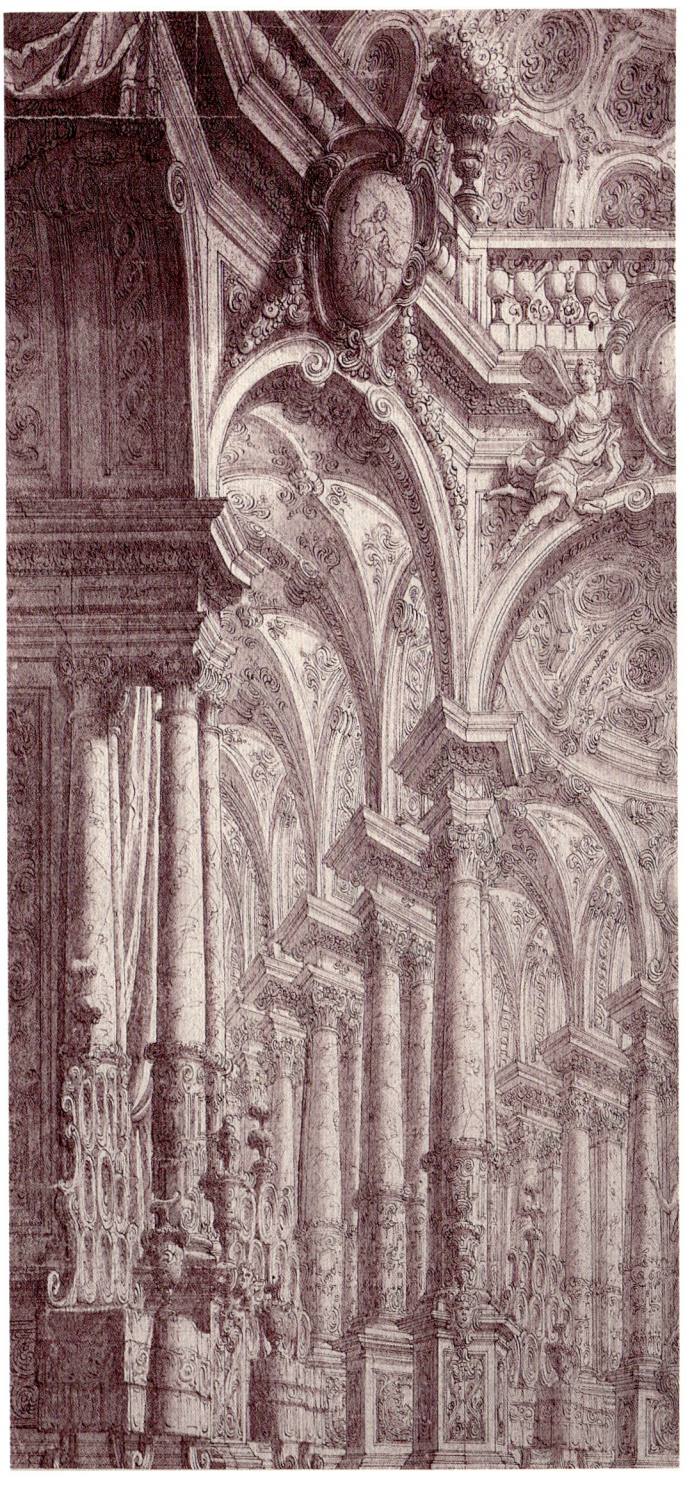

29. Francesco Bibiena, *"Grand Imperial Loggia,"* Act 1, Scene 1, pen and ink with sepia wash

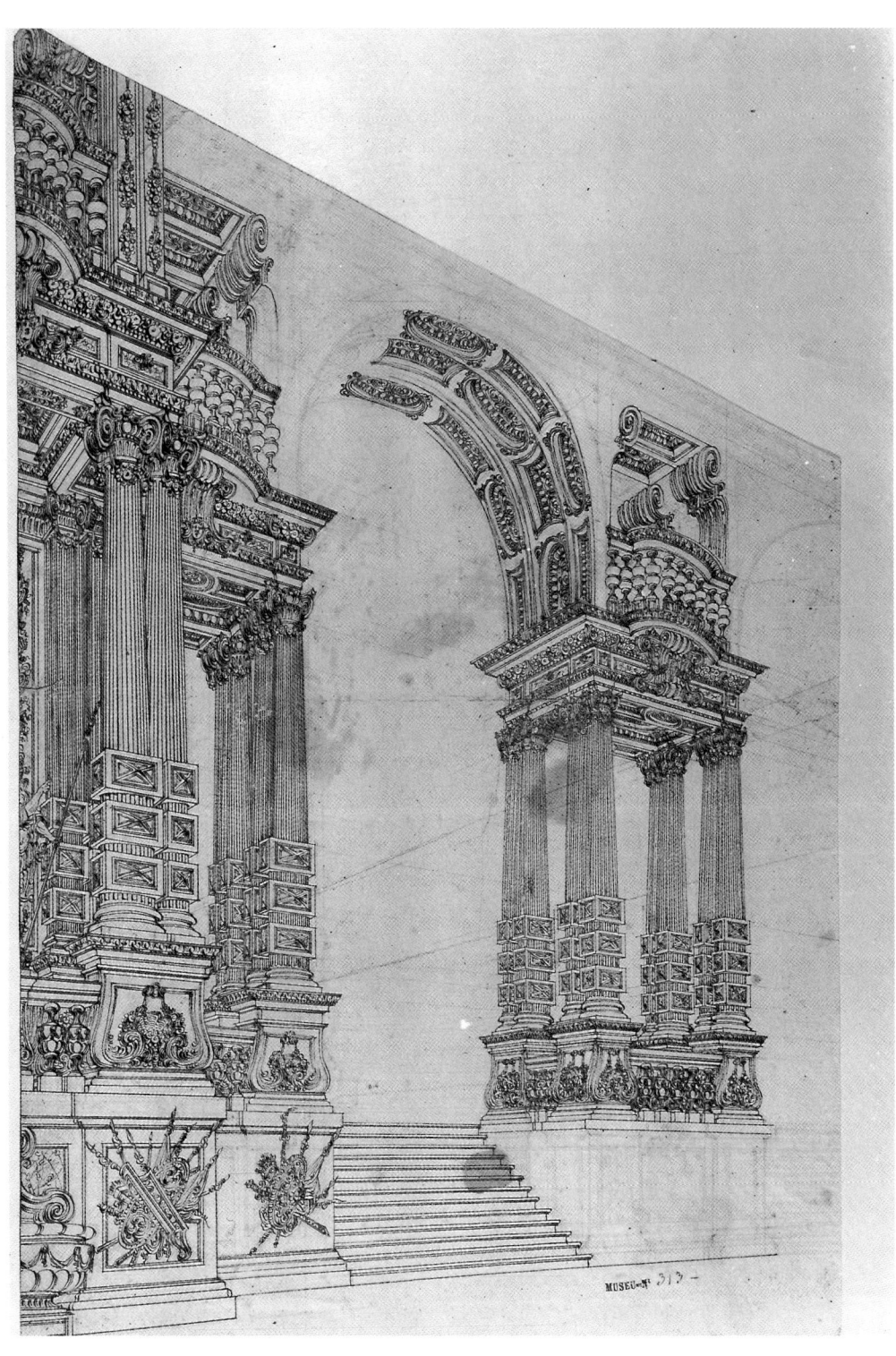

30. Francesco Bibiena, *Portion of a Stage Design with Columns and Staircases "Per un Trionfo,"* pen and ink with sepia wash

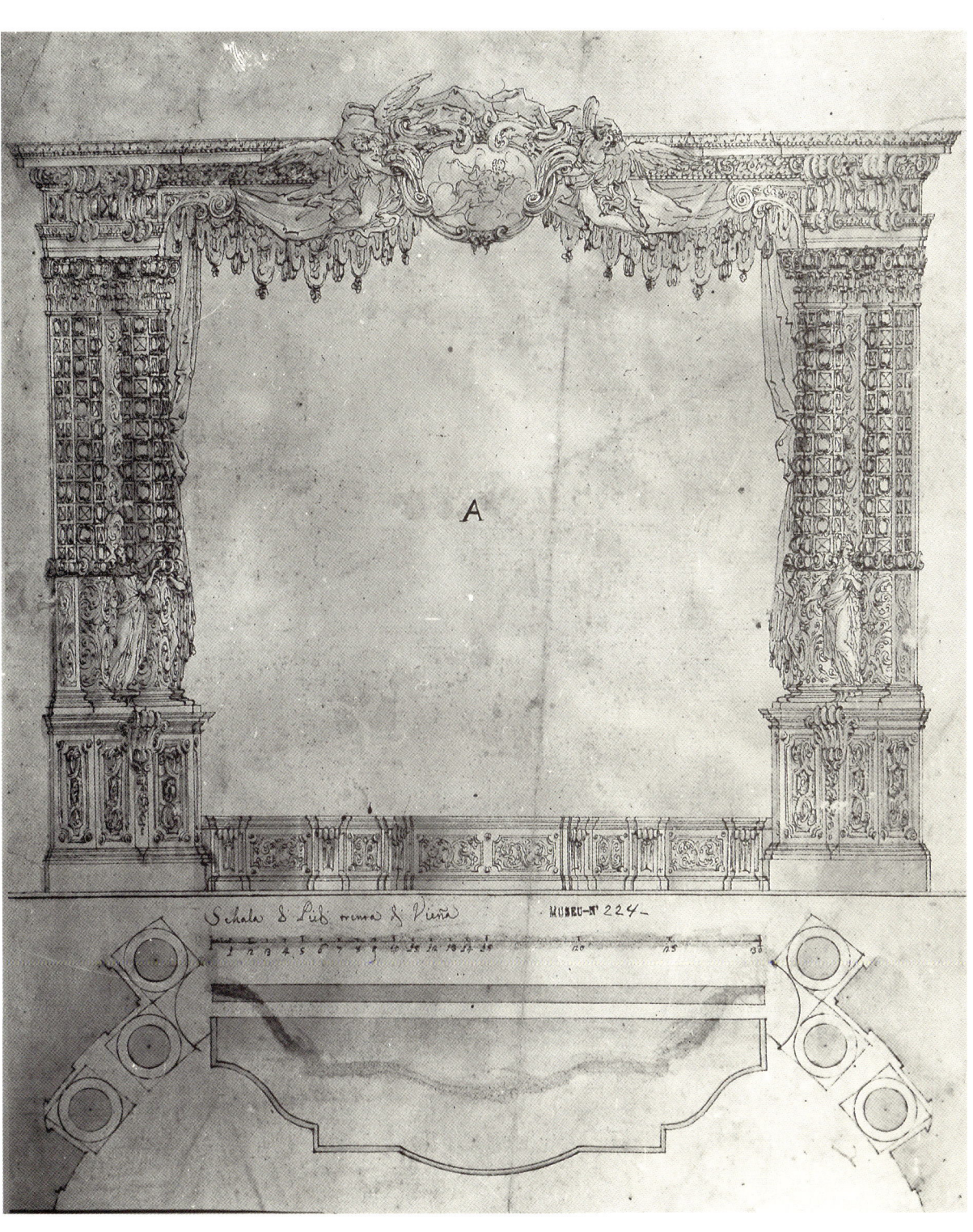

31. Francesco Bibiena, *Theater of Vienna Proscenium, Plan, and Elevation*, pen and ink, bistre, and sepia

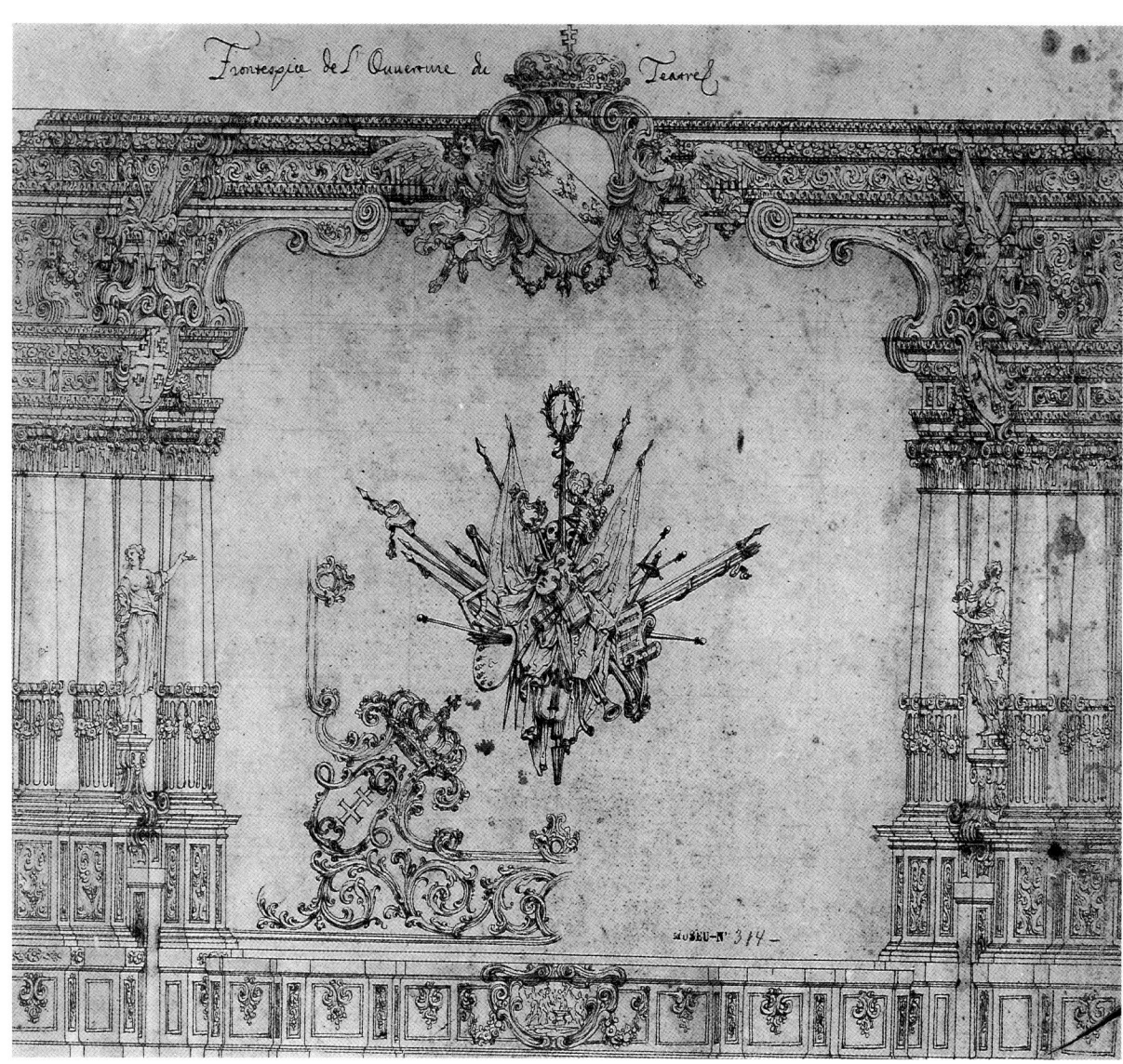

32. Francesco Bibiena, *Proscenium*, pen and ink bistre with sepia wash

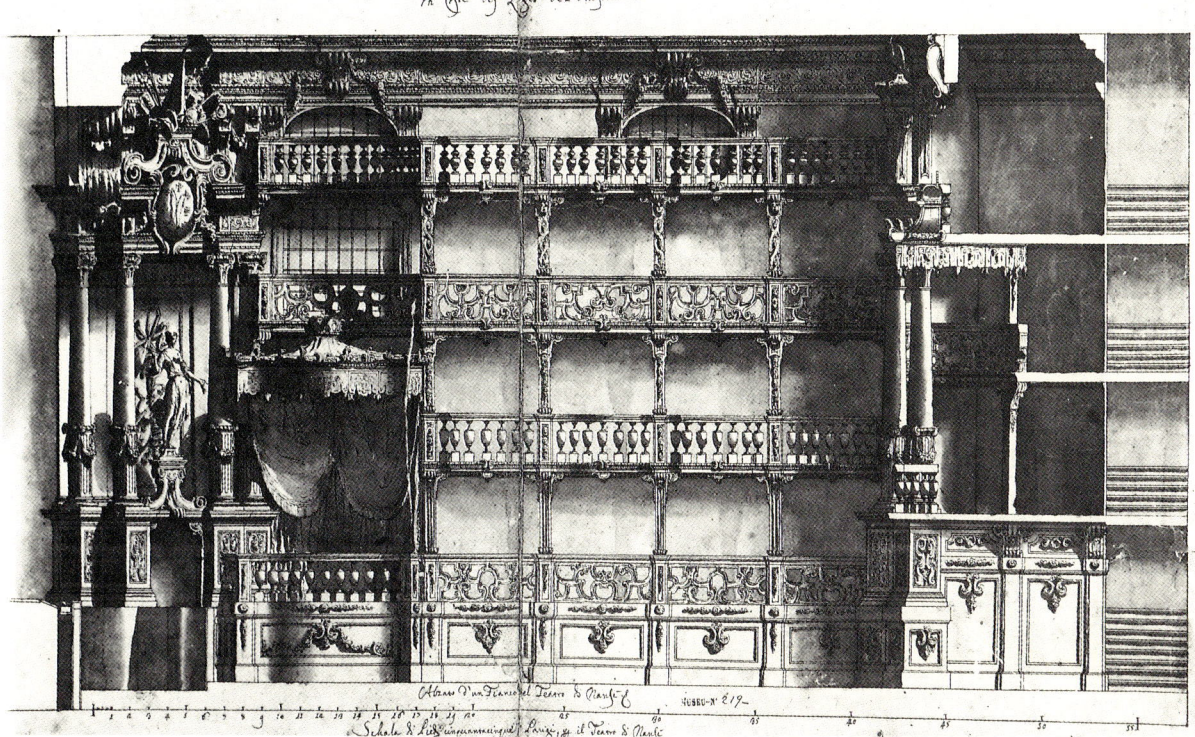

33. Francesco Bibiena, *Vertical Projections Flanking the Stage*, pen and ink bistre with sepia wash

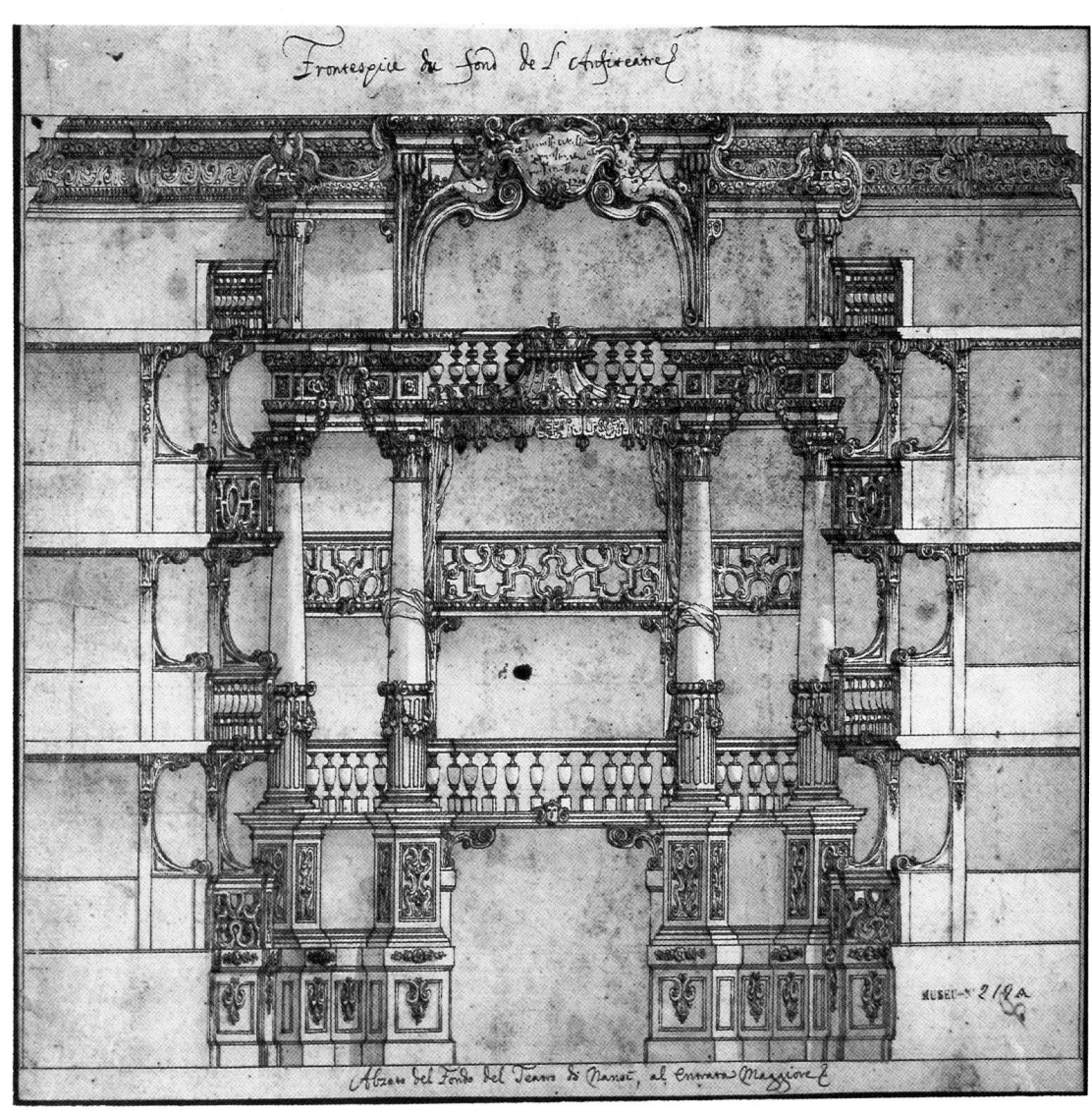

34. Francesco Bibiena, *Elevation of the Theater Boxes Facing the Stage, dated 1708*, pen and ink bistre with sepia wash

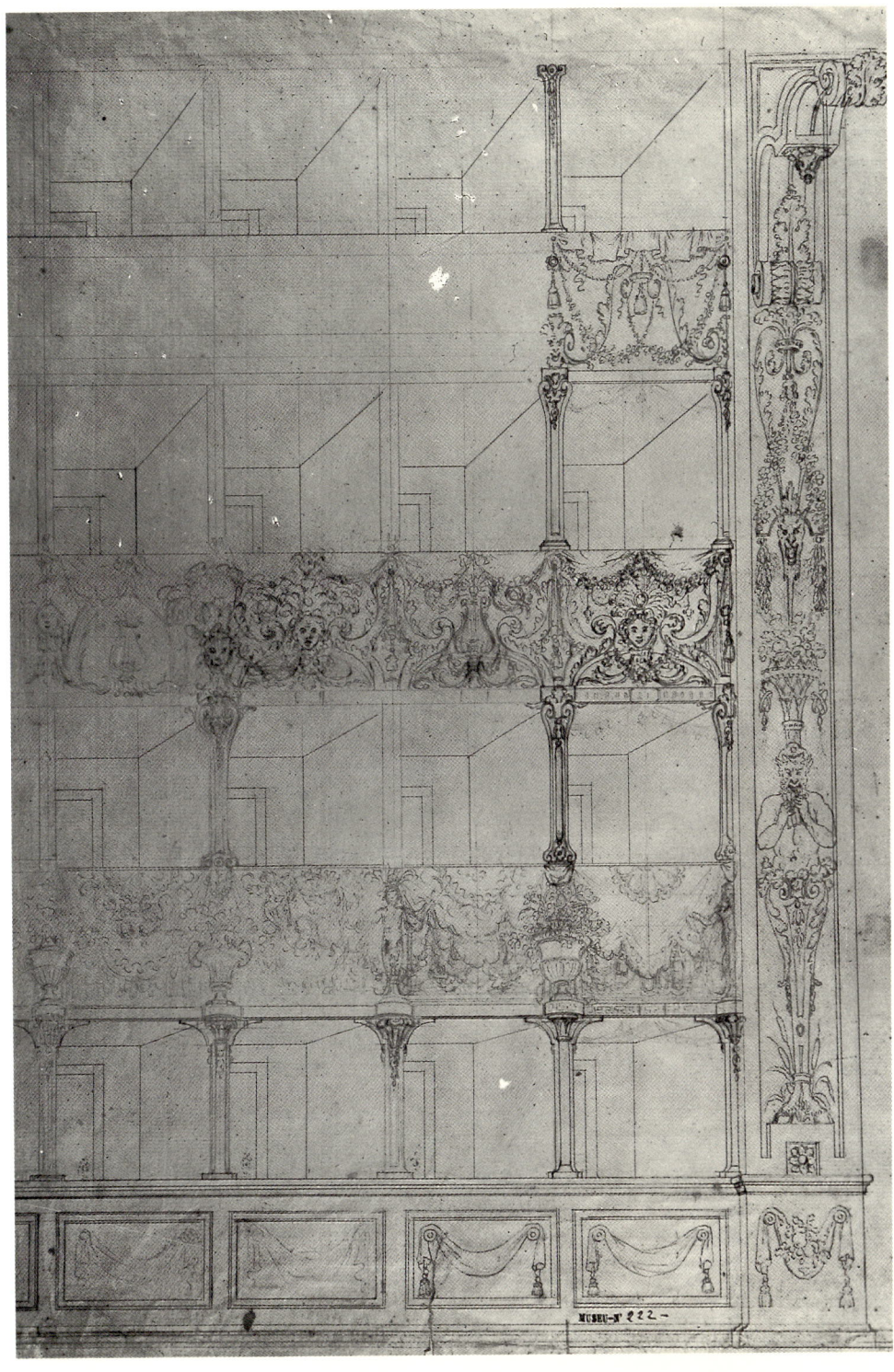

35. Francesco Bibiena, *Elevation with Four Rows of Theater Boxes*, pencil

54

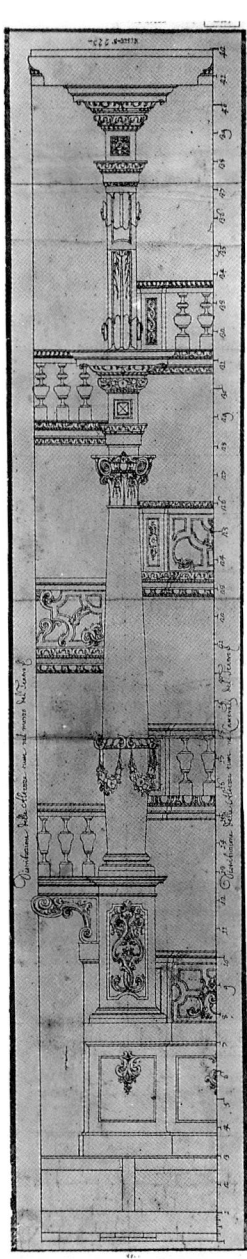

36. Francesco Bibiena, *Study for Theater Boxes*, pen and bistre

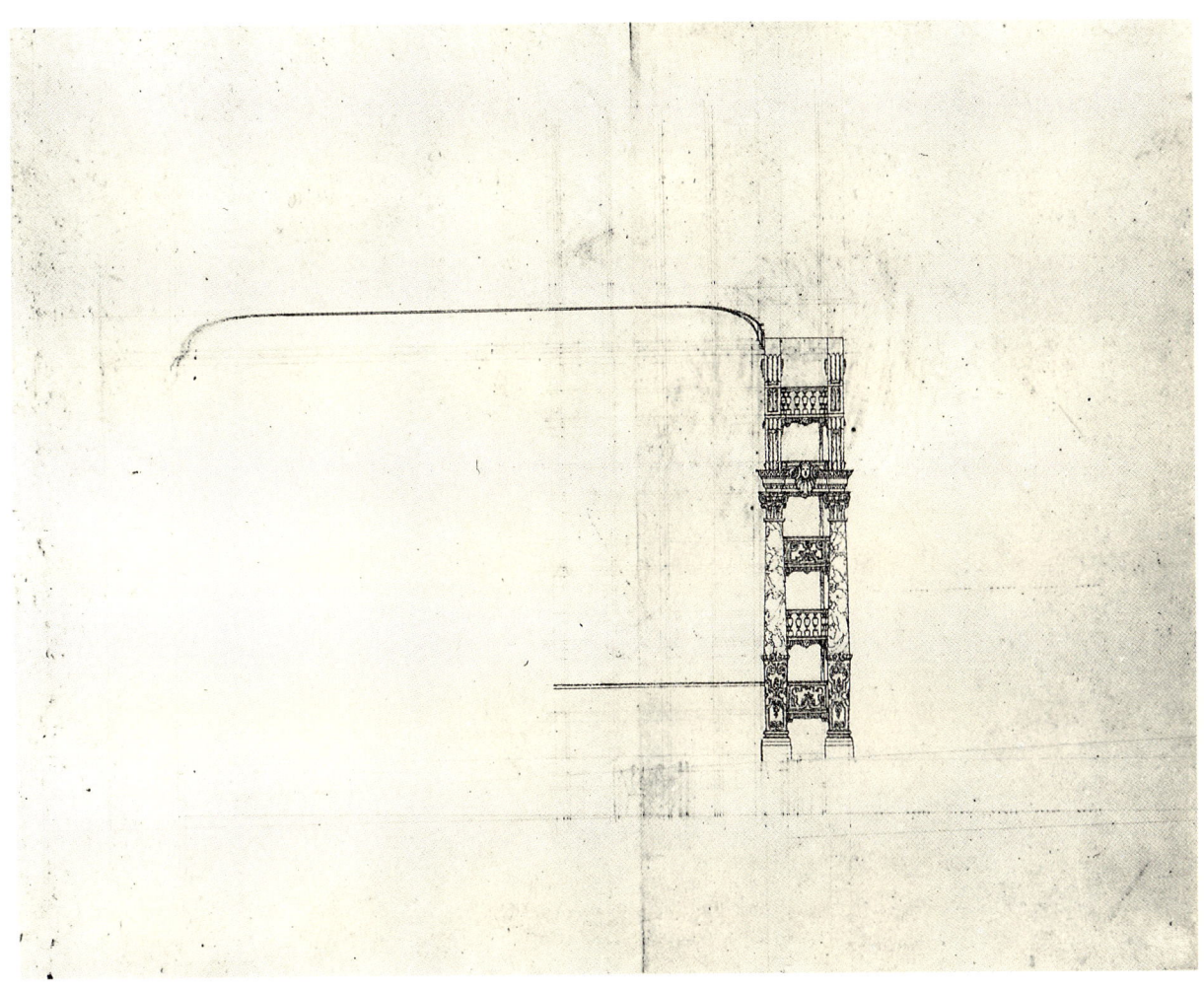

37. Francesco Bibiena, *Sketch for Proscenium and Theater Boxes*, pen and ink with sepia wash

56

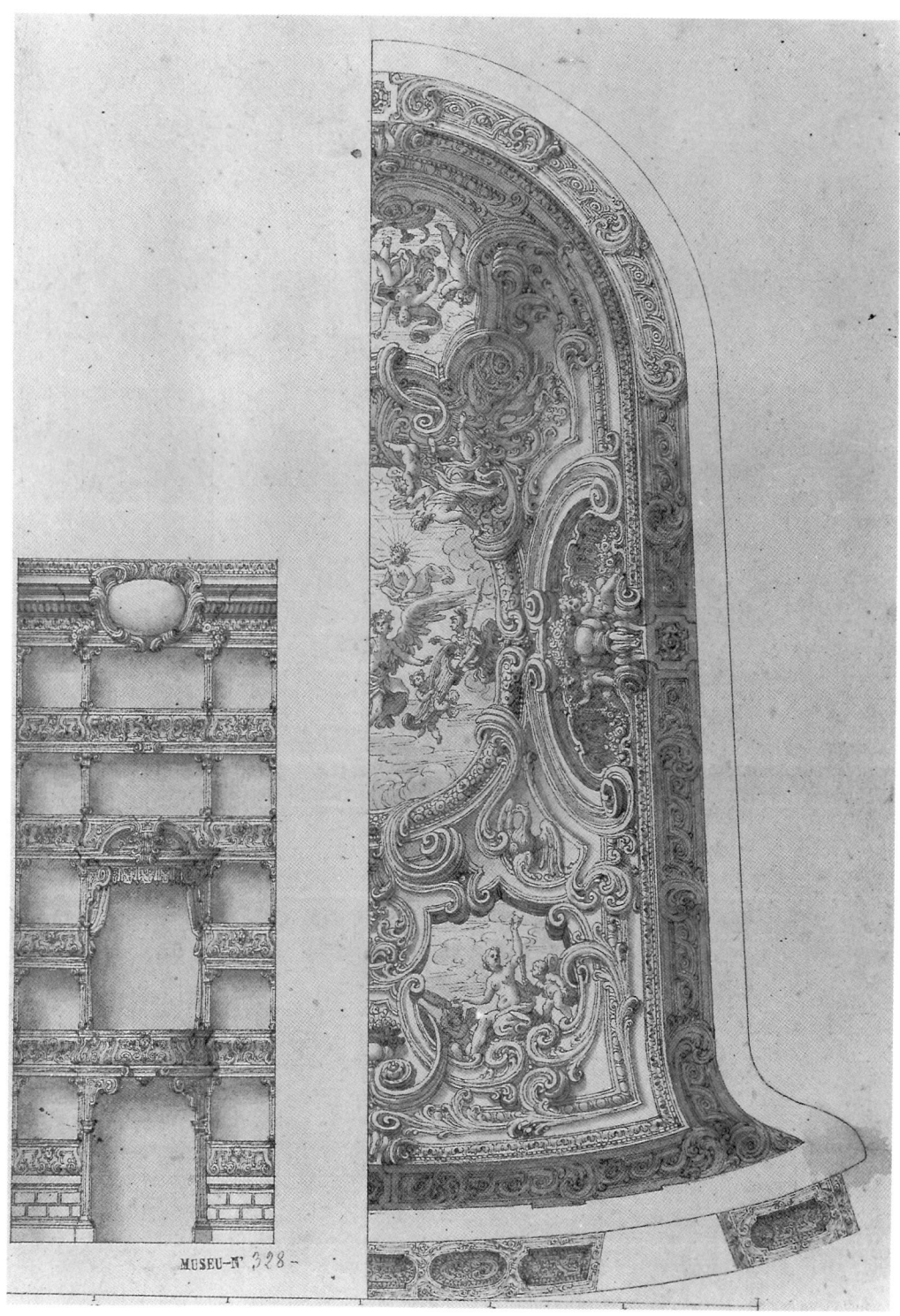

38. Francesco Bibiena, *Part of the Bell-Shaped Ceiling with Five Rows of Theater Boxes and the Stage*, pen and ink bistre with sepia wash

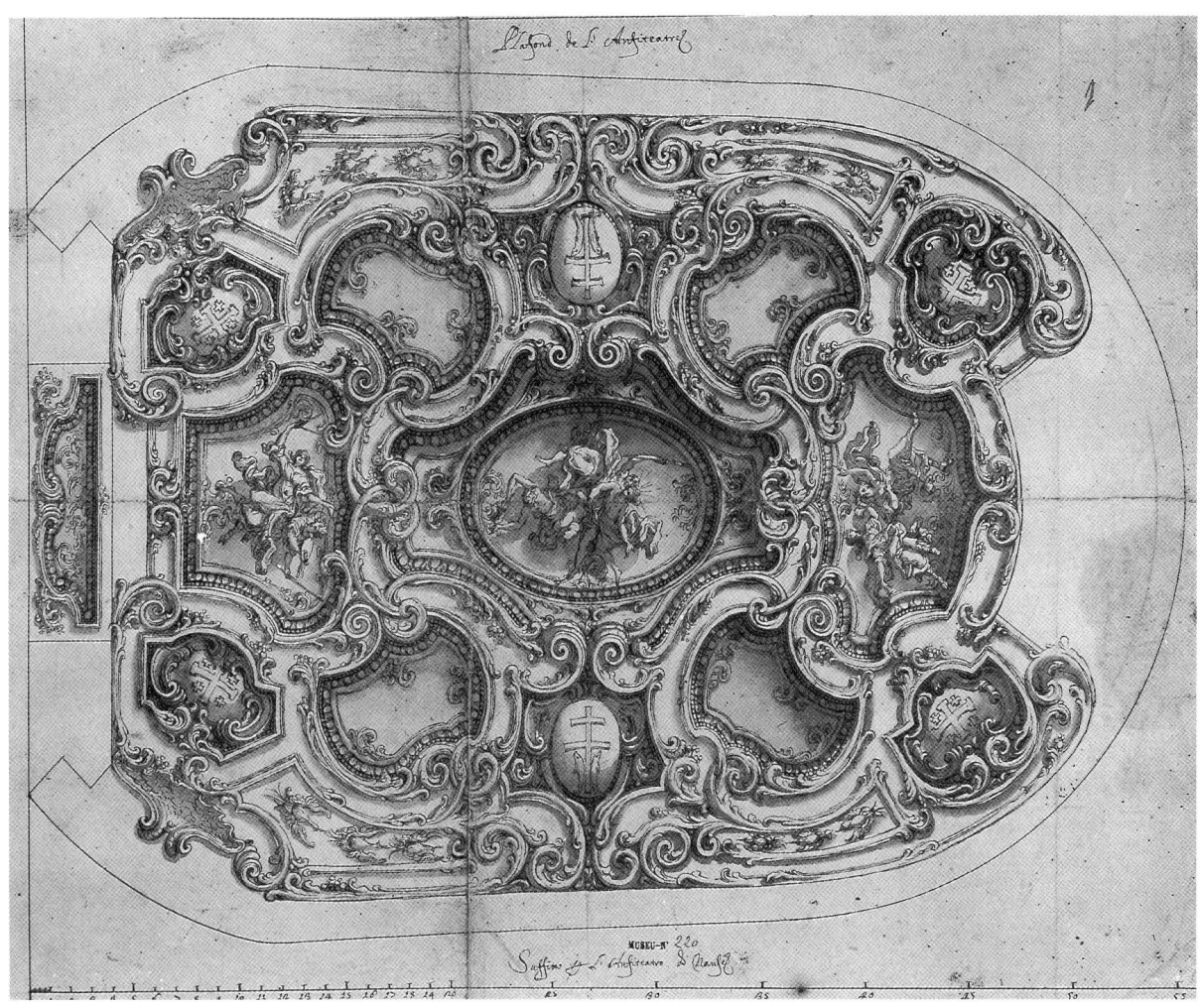

39. Francesco Bibiena, *Decoration for the Ceiling*, pen and ink bistre with sepia wash

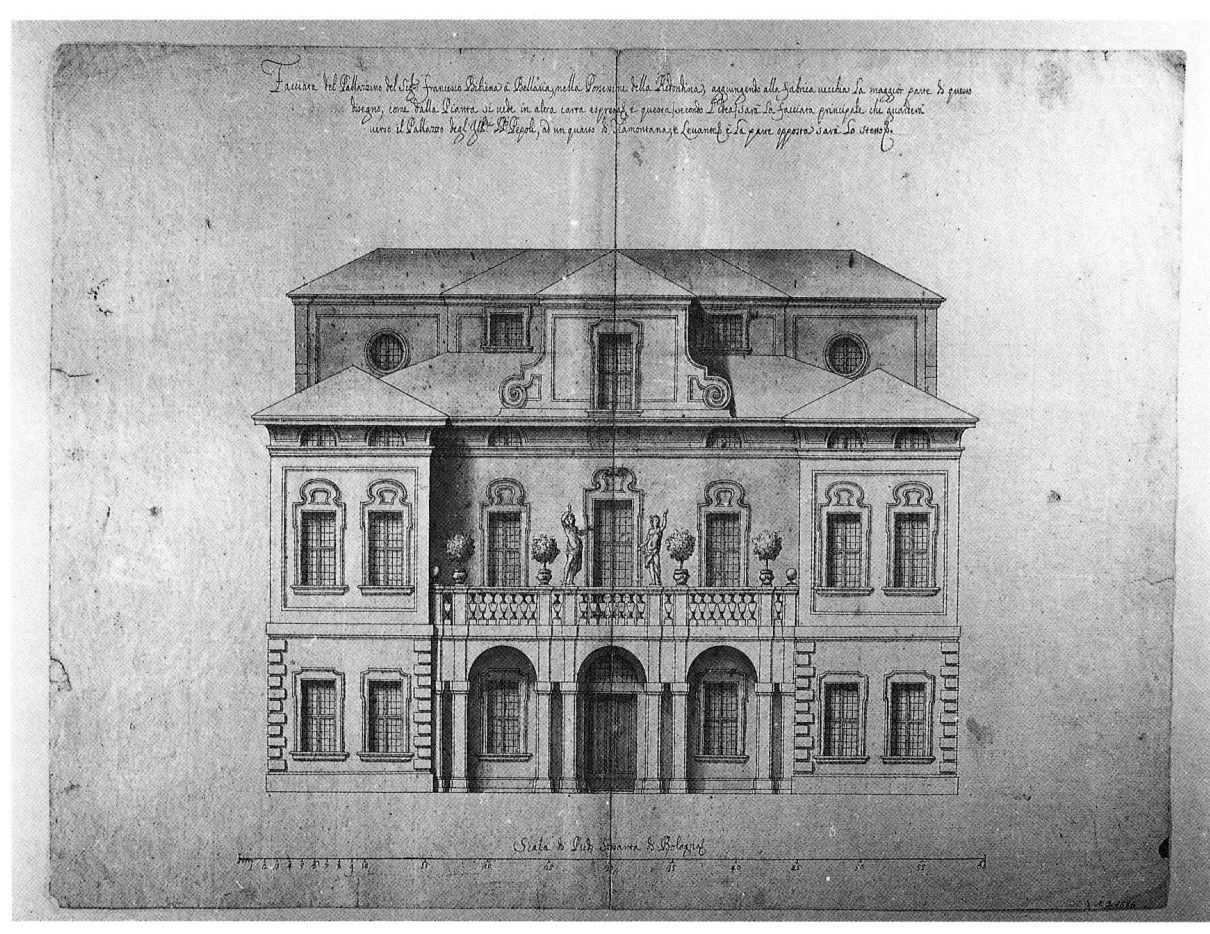

40. Francesco Bibiena, *Main Facade*, pen and ink with sepia wash

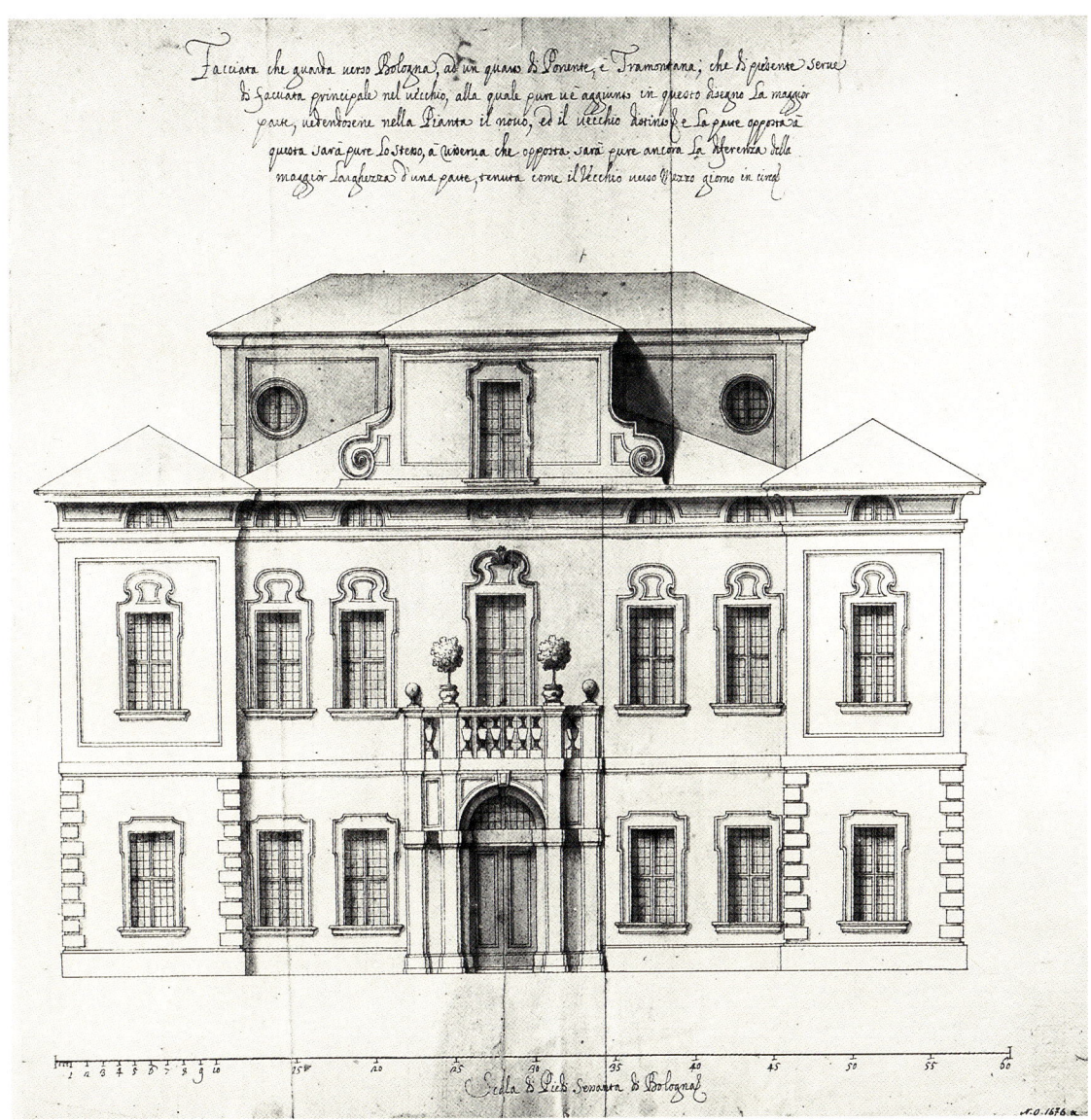

41. Francesco Bibiena, *Lateral Facade*, pen and ink with sepia wash

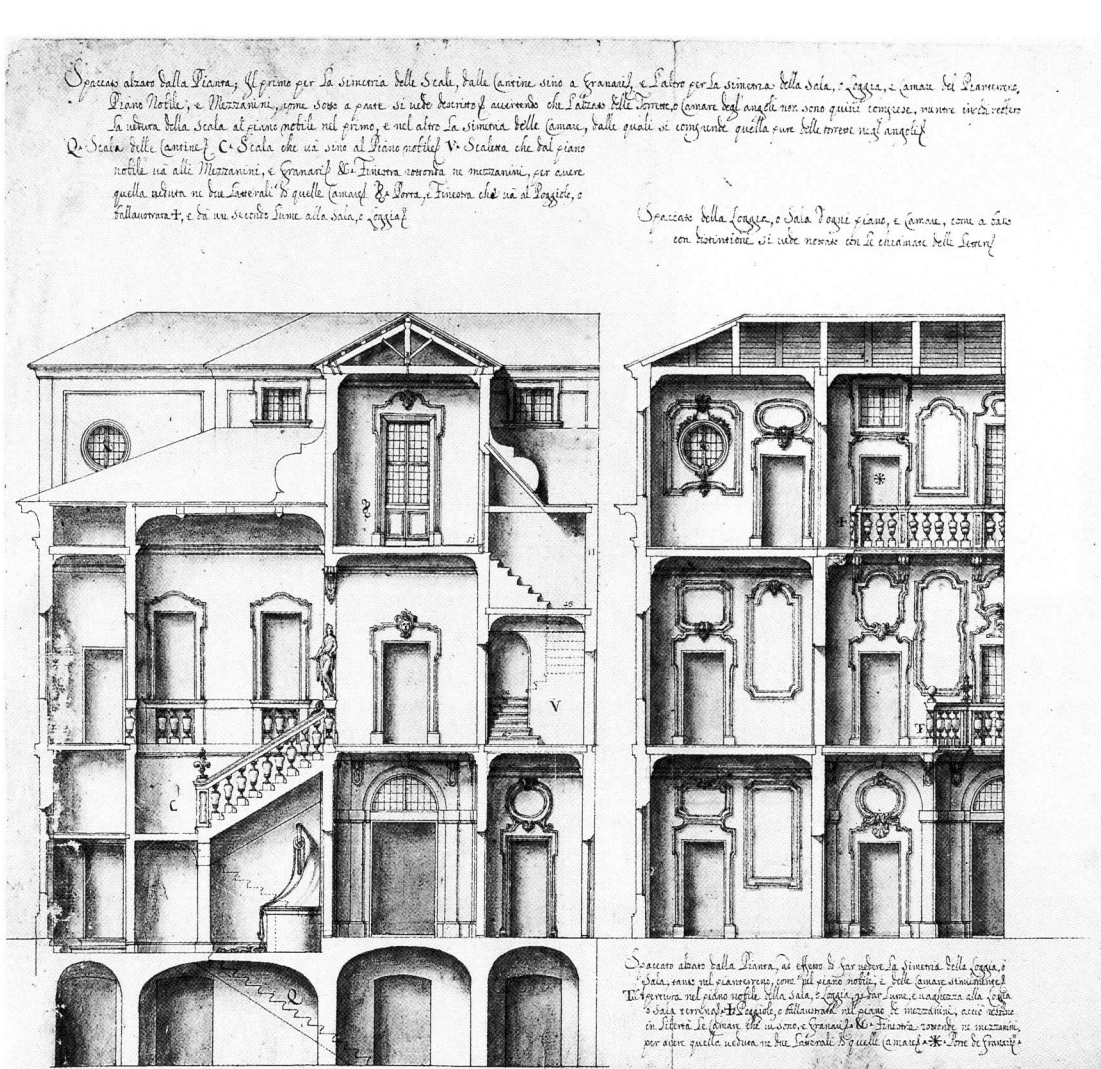

42. Francesco Bibiena, *Elevations for Two Corresponding Designs*, pen and ink bistre with sepia wash

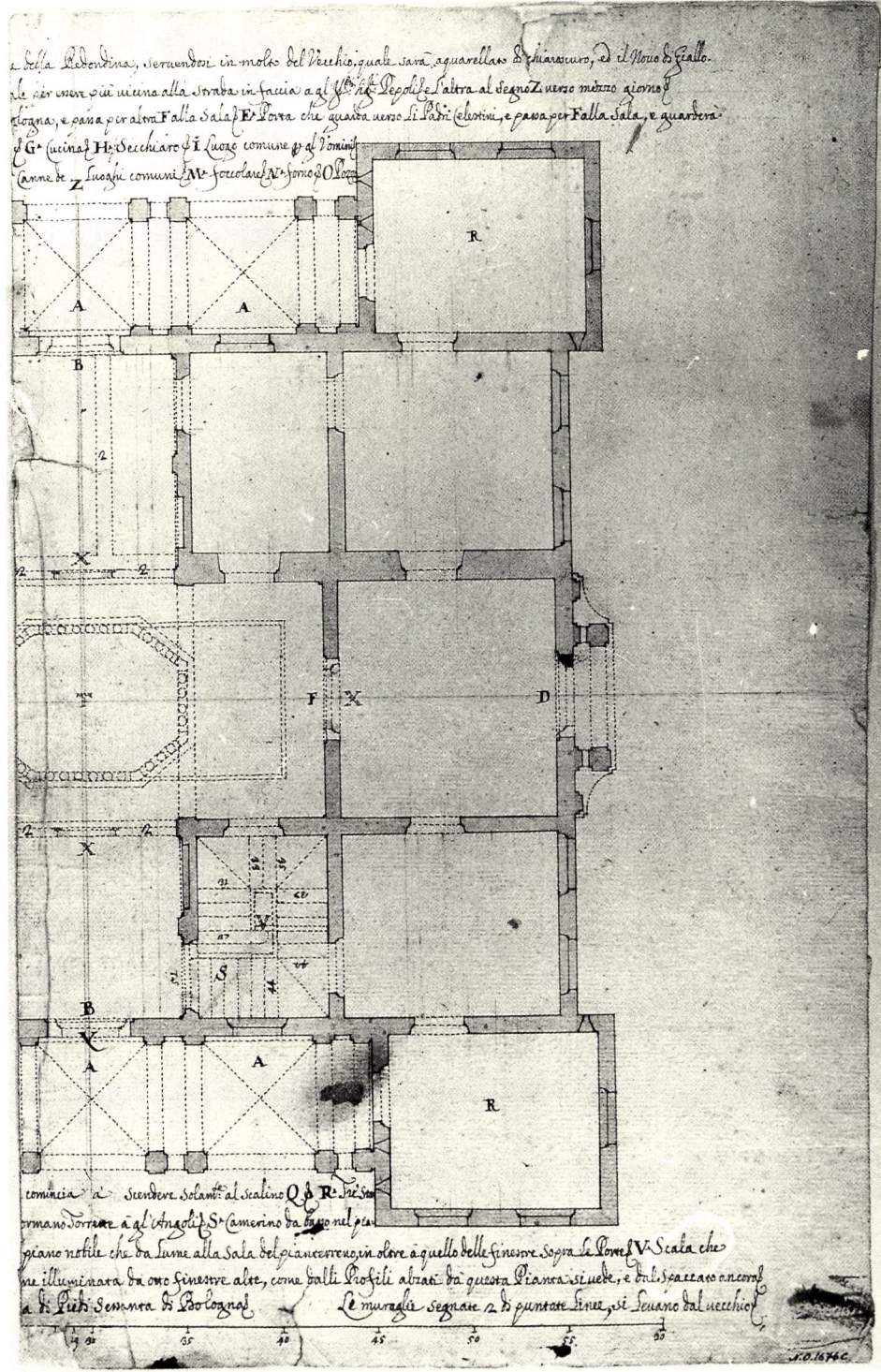

43. Francesco Bibiena, *Plan Corresponding to the Lateral Facade*, pen and ink bistre with sepia wash

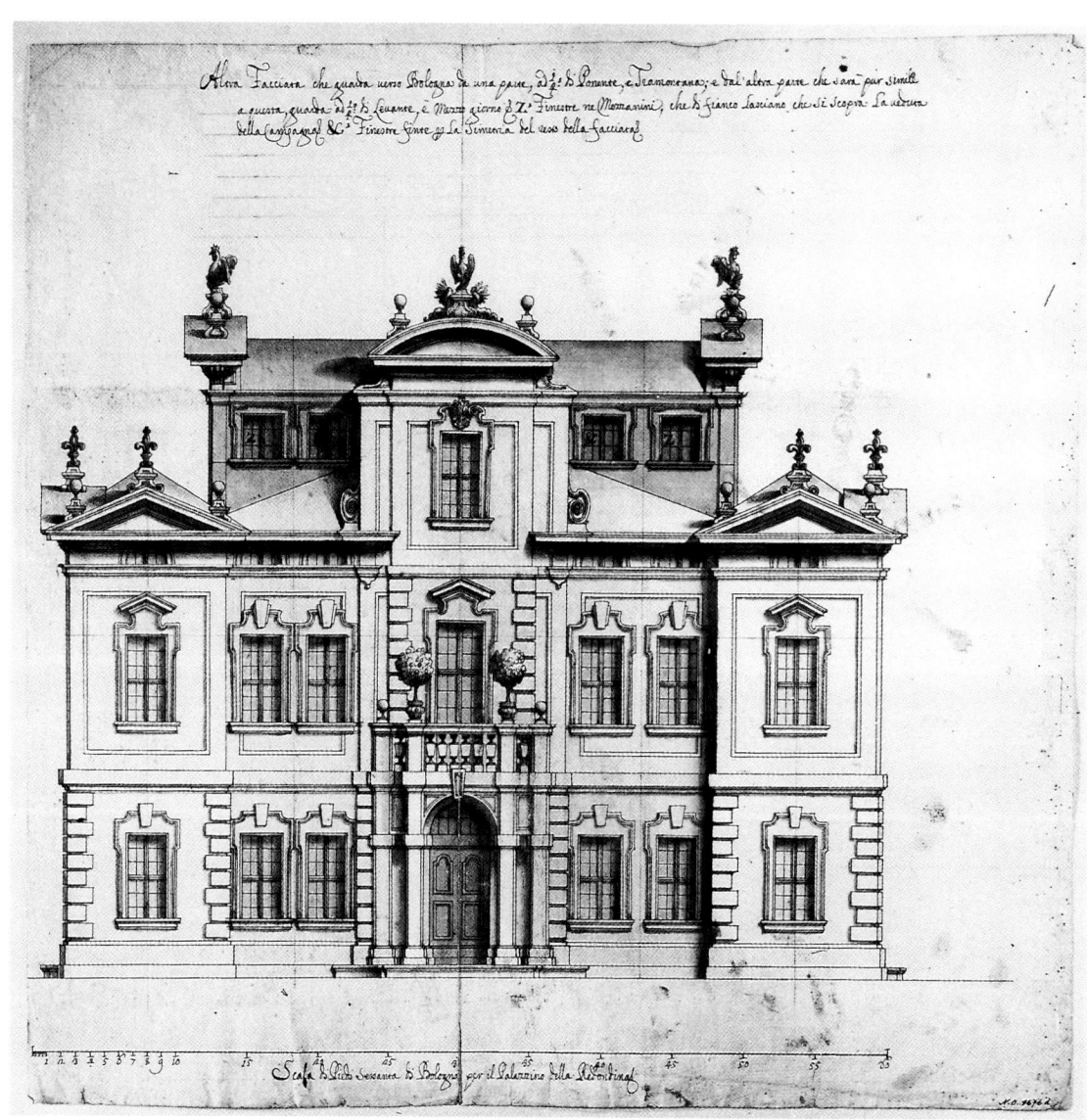

44. Francesco Bibiena, *Lateral Facade*, pen and ink bistre with sepia wash

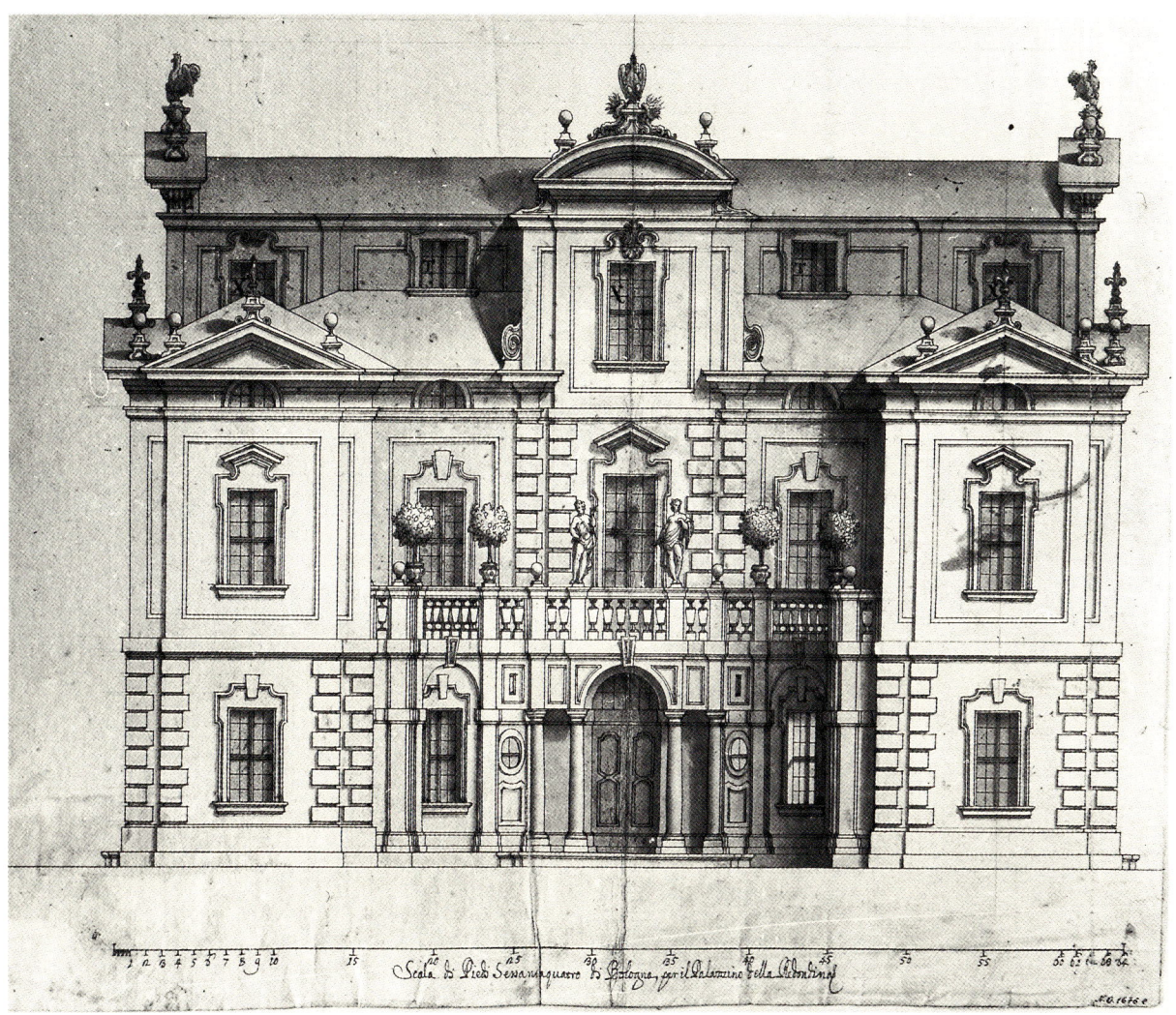

45. Francesco Bibiena, *Main Facade*, pen and ink bistre with sepia wash

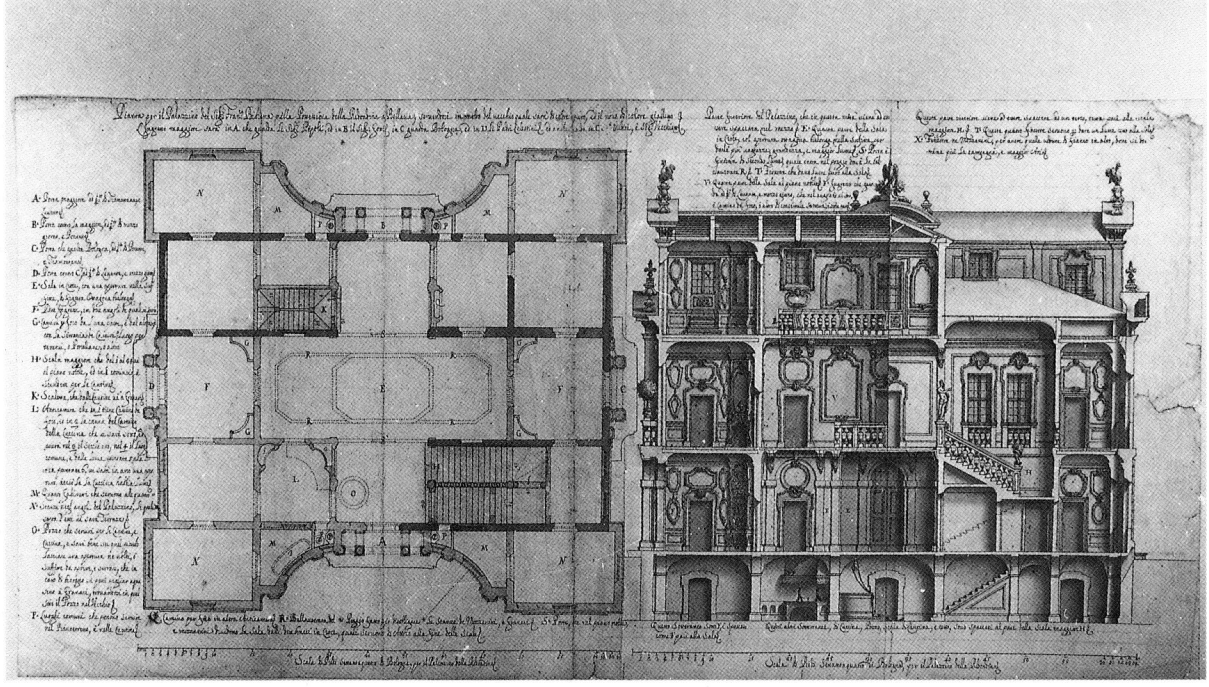

46. Francesco Bibiena, *Plan of the Residence with Two Corresponding Designs*, pen and ink with sepia wash

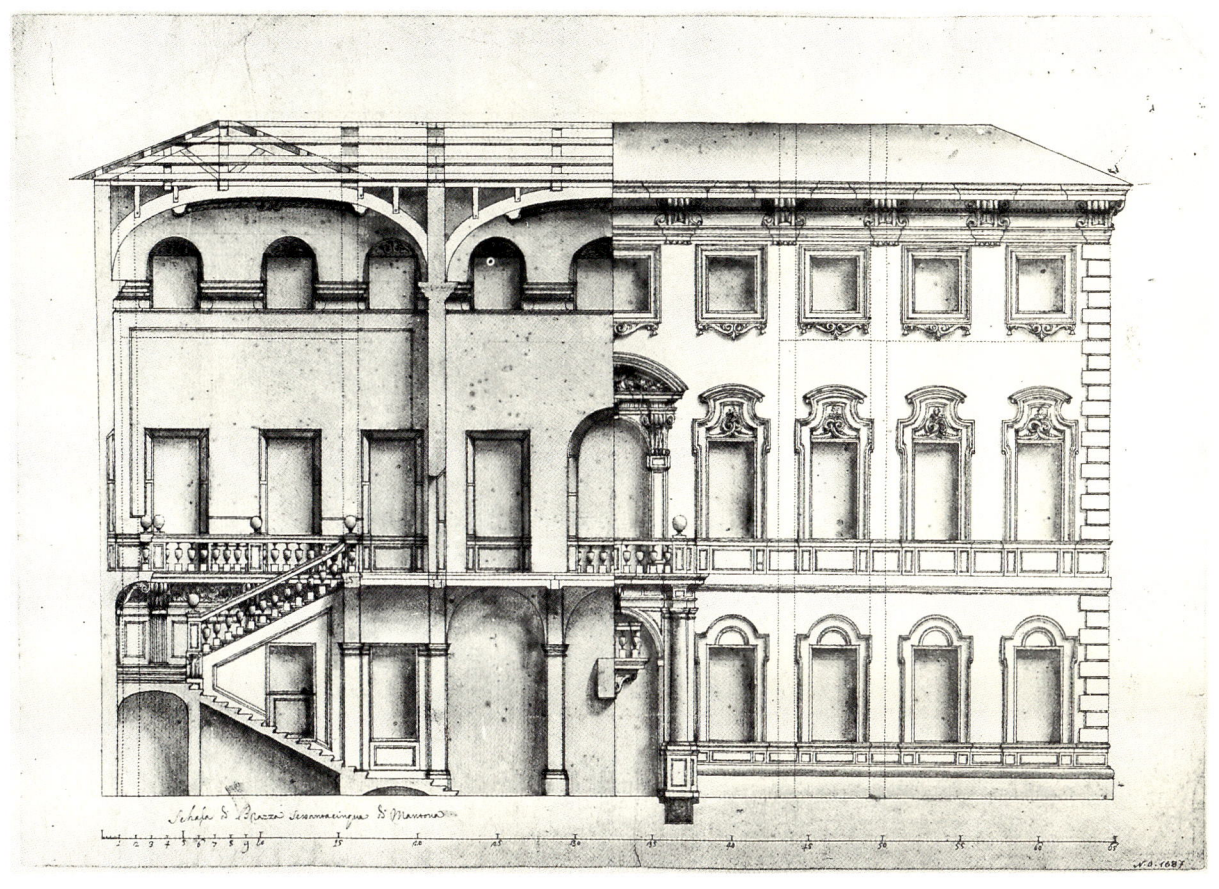

47. Francesco Bibiena, *Building in Mantua*, pen and ink with sepia and pink wash

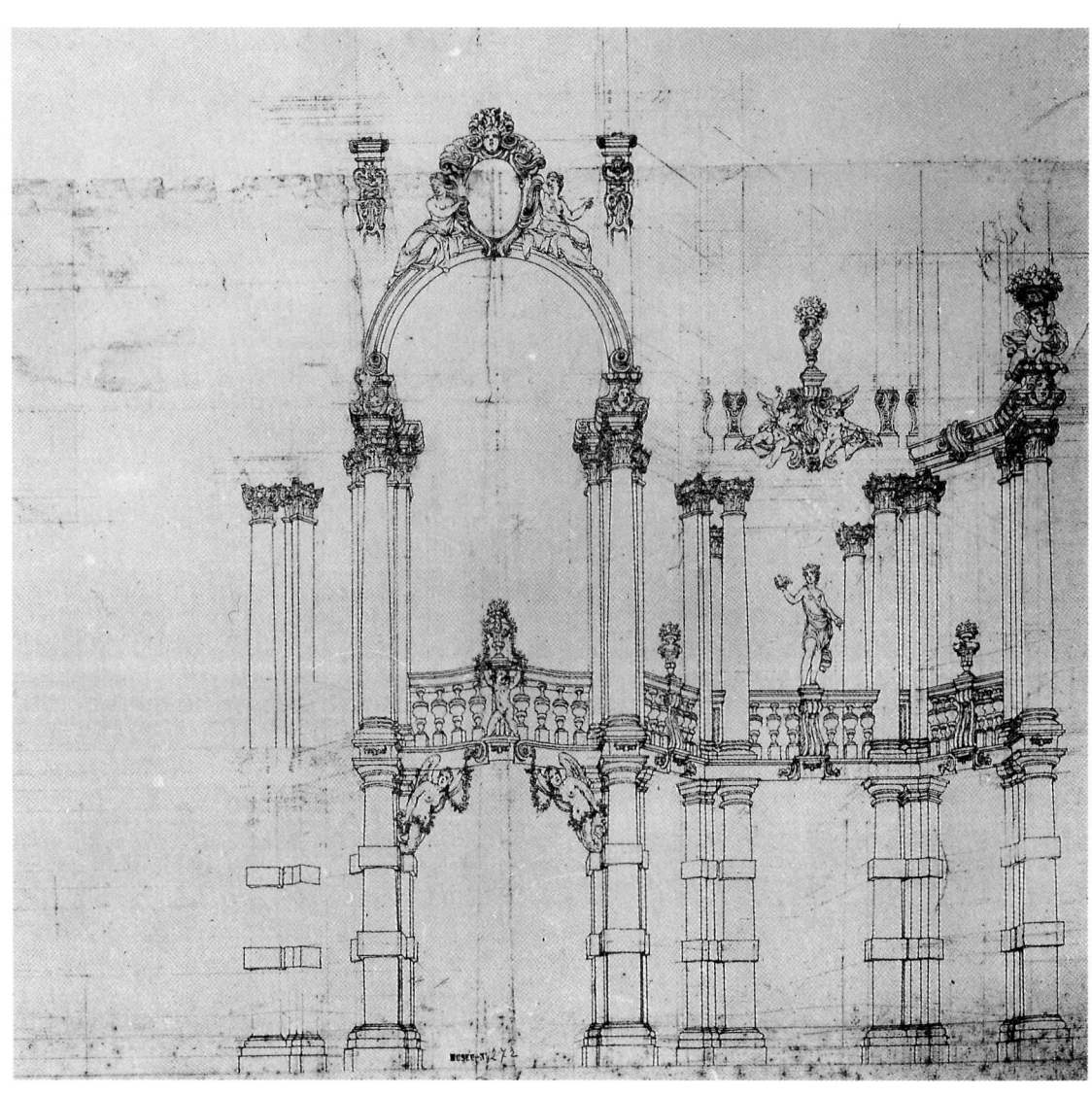

48. Francesco Bibiena, *Plan for Decorative Architecture*, pen and ink with sepia wash

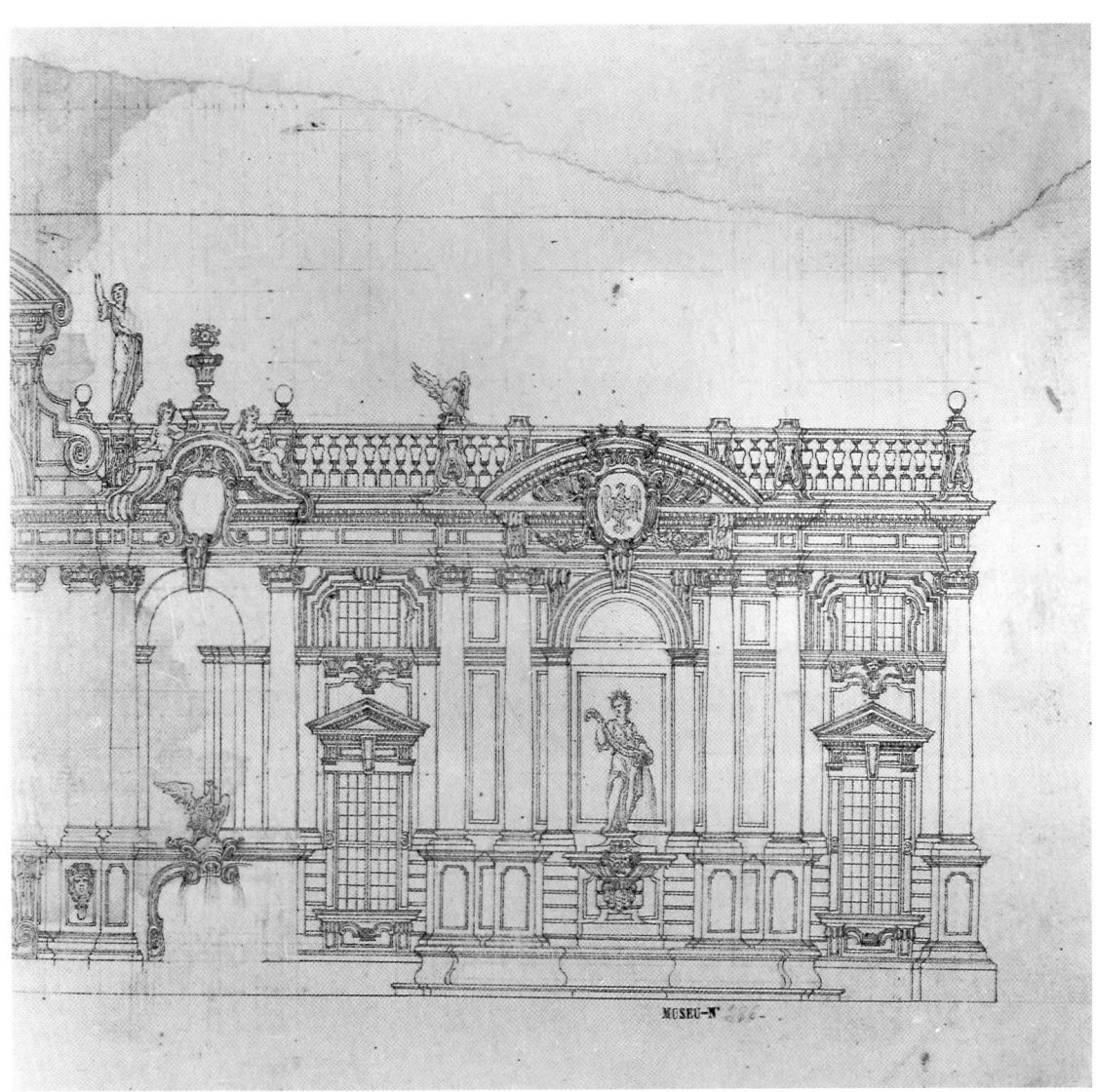

49. Francesco Bibiena, *Facade for a Palace*, pen and ink with sepia wash

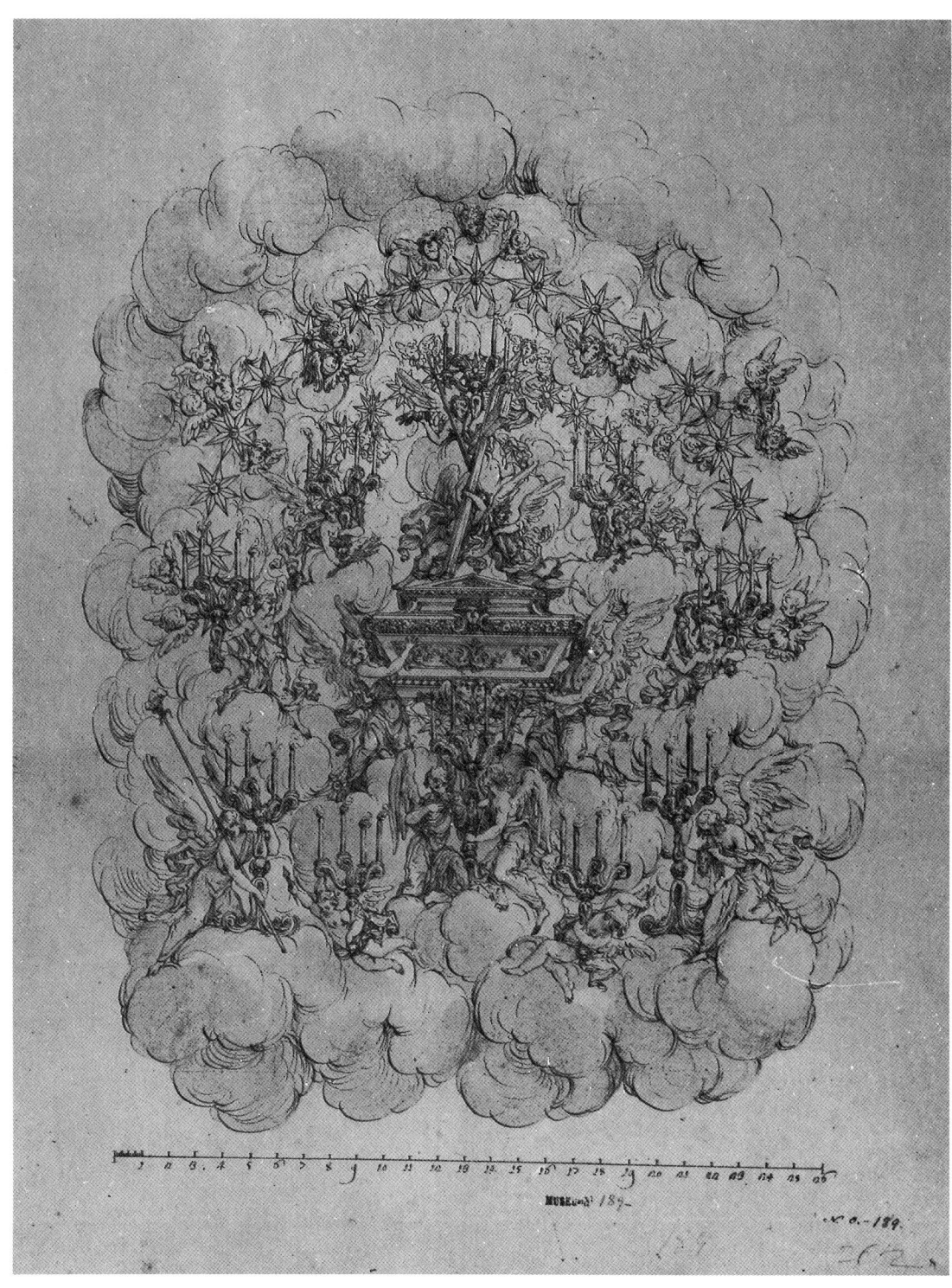

50. Francesco Bibiena, *Scenographic Composition with Symbols of the Passion of Christ*, pen and ink with sepia wash

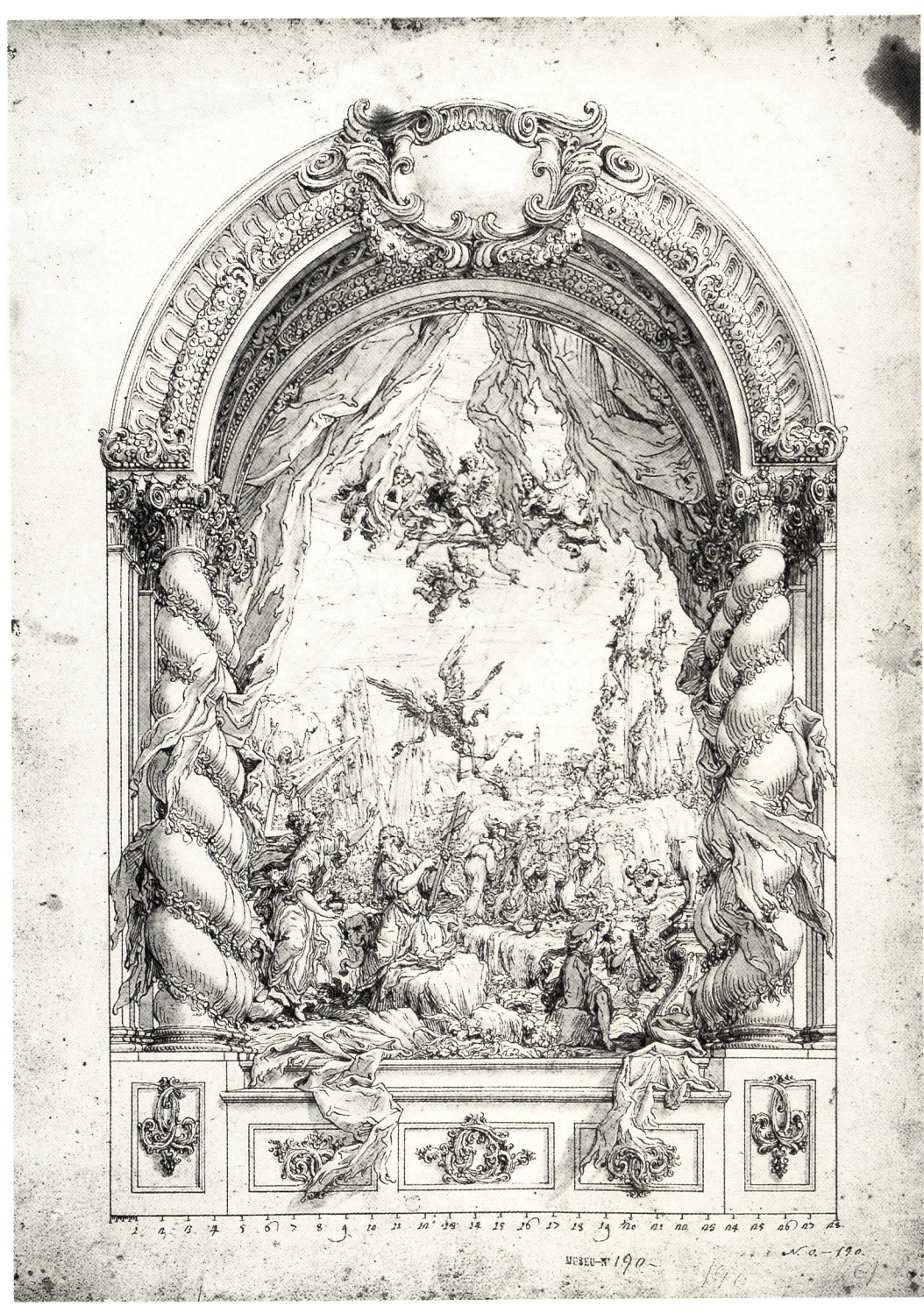

51. Francesco Bibiena, *Composition for an Altarpiece Alluding to Death*, pen and ink with sepia wash

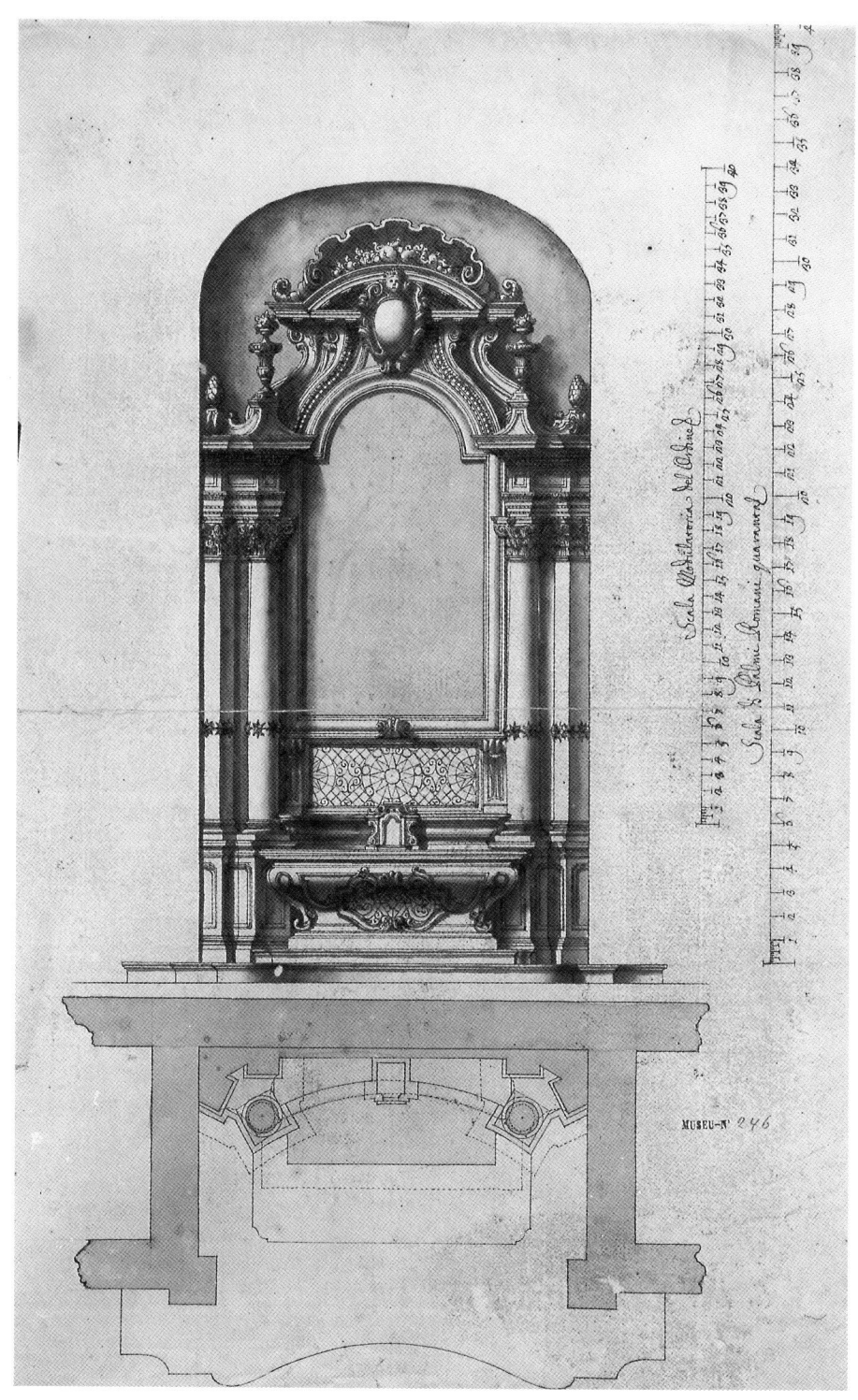

52. Francesco Bibiena, *Project for an Altar Elevation*, pen and ink with sepia wash

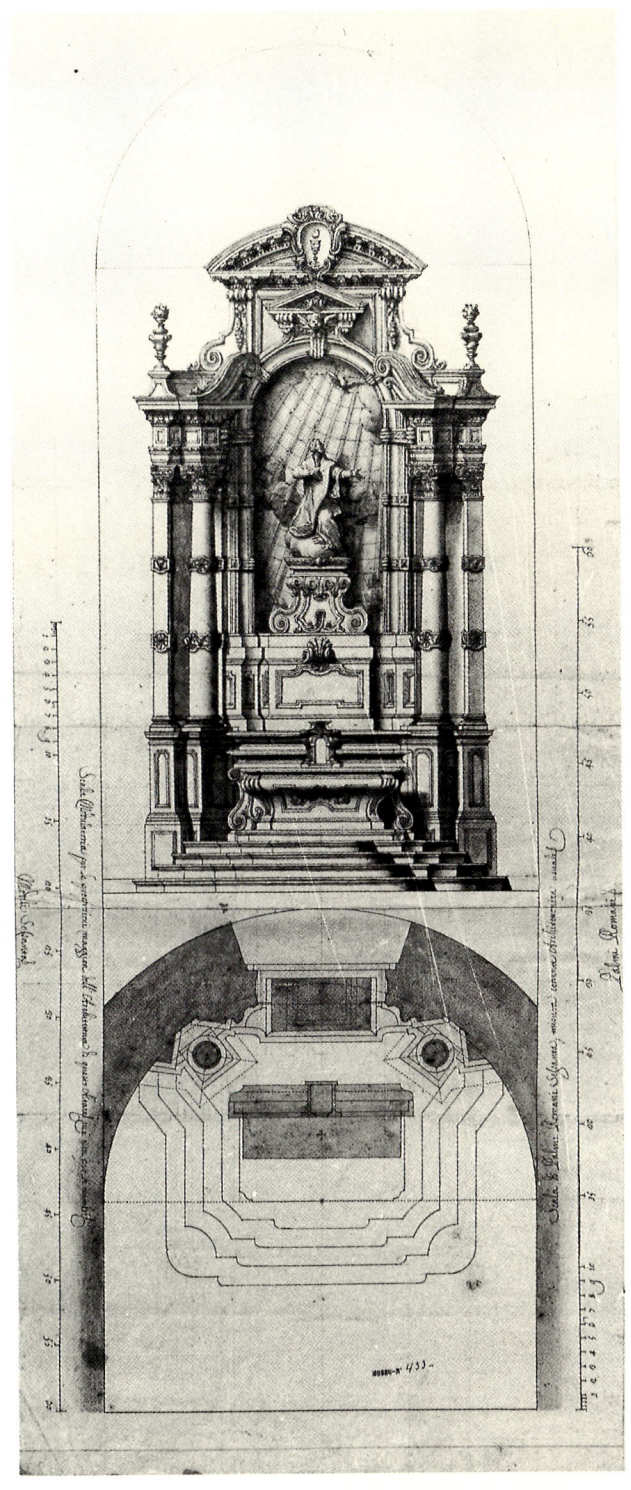

53. Francesco Bibiena, *Elevation and Plan for an Altar with the Image of a Pious Saint*, pen and ink with greenish brown wash

72

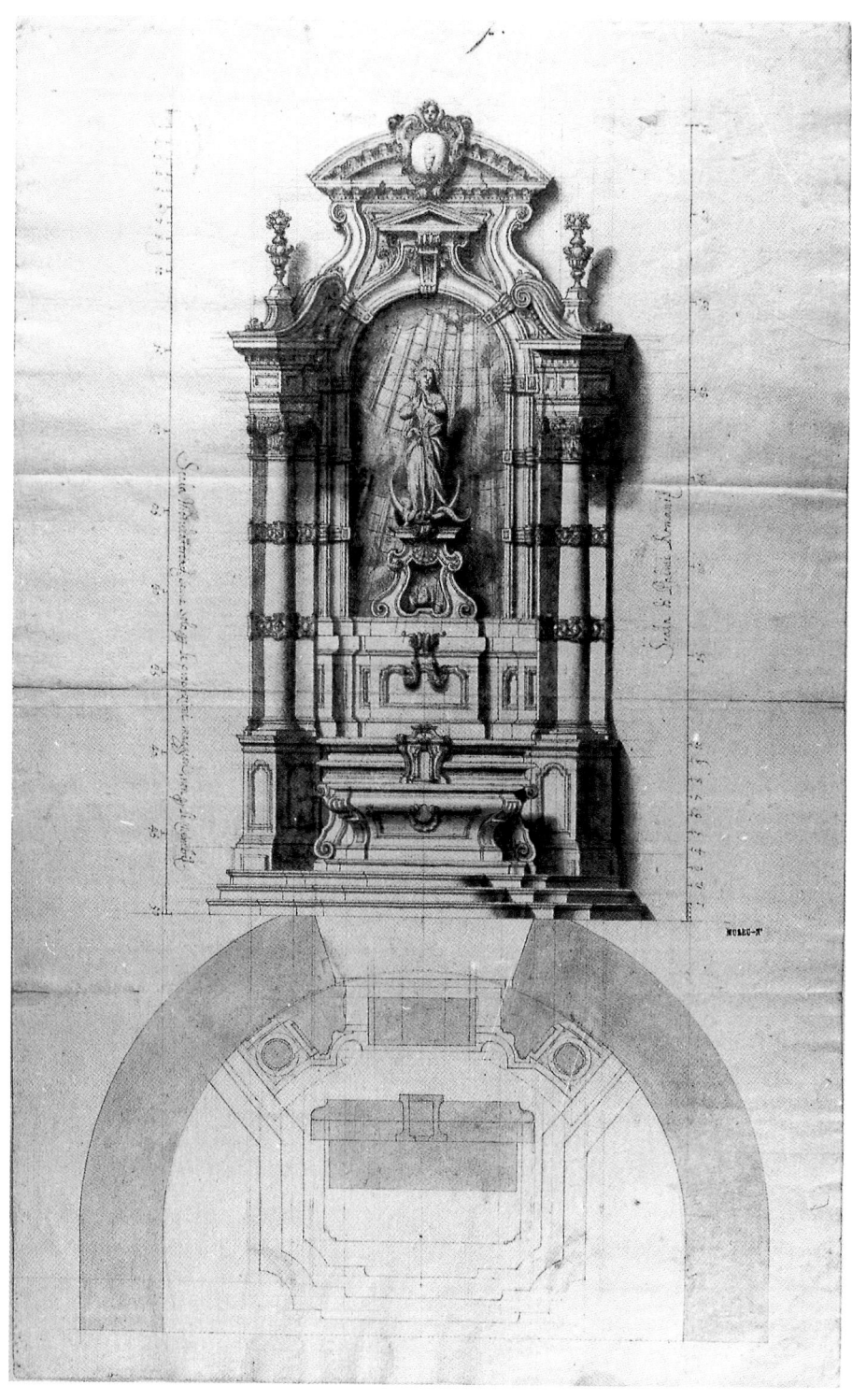

54. Francesco Bibiena, *Elevation and Plan for an Altar with the Image of Our Lady of the Assumption*, pen and ink with brown and greenish gray wash

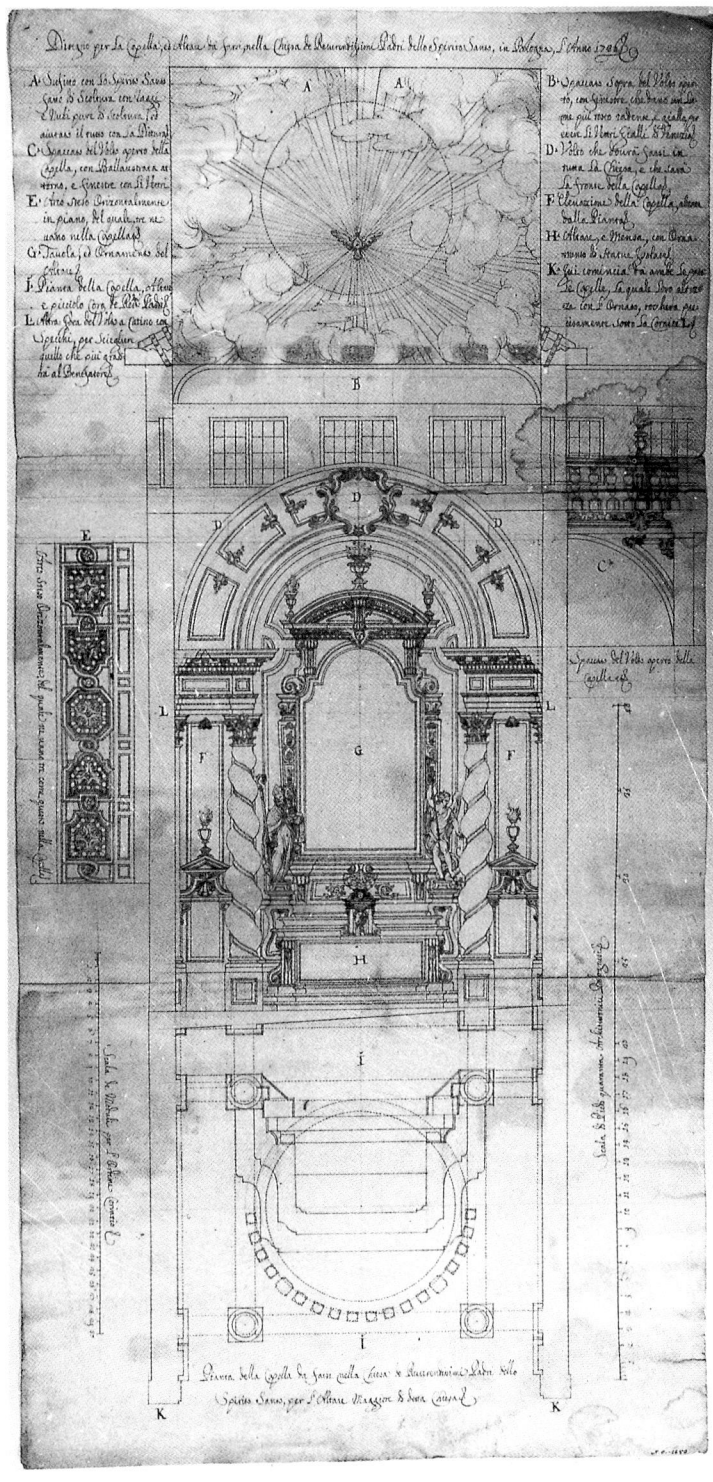

55. Francesco Bibiena, *Elevation and Plan for an Altar of the Church of the Holy Spirit in Bologna*, pen and ink with sepia wash

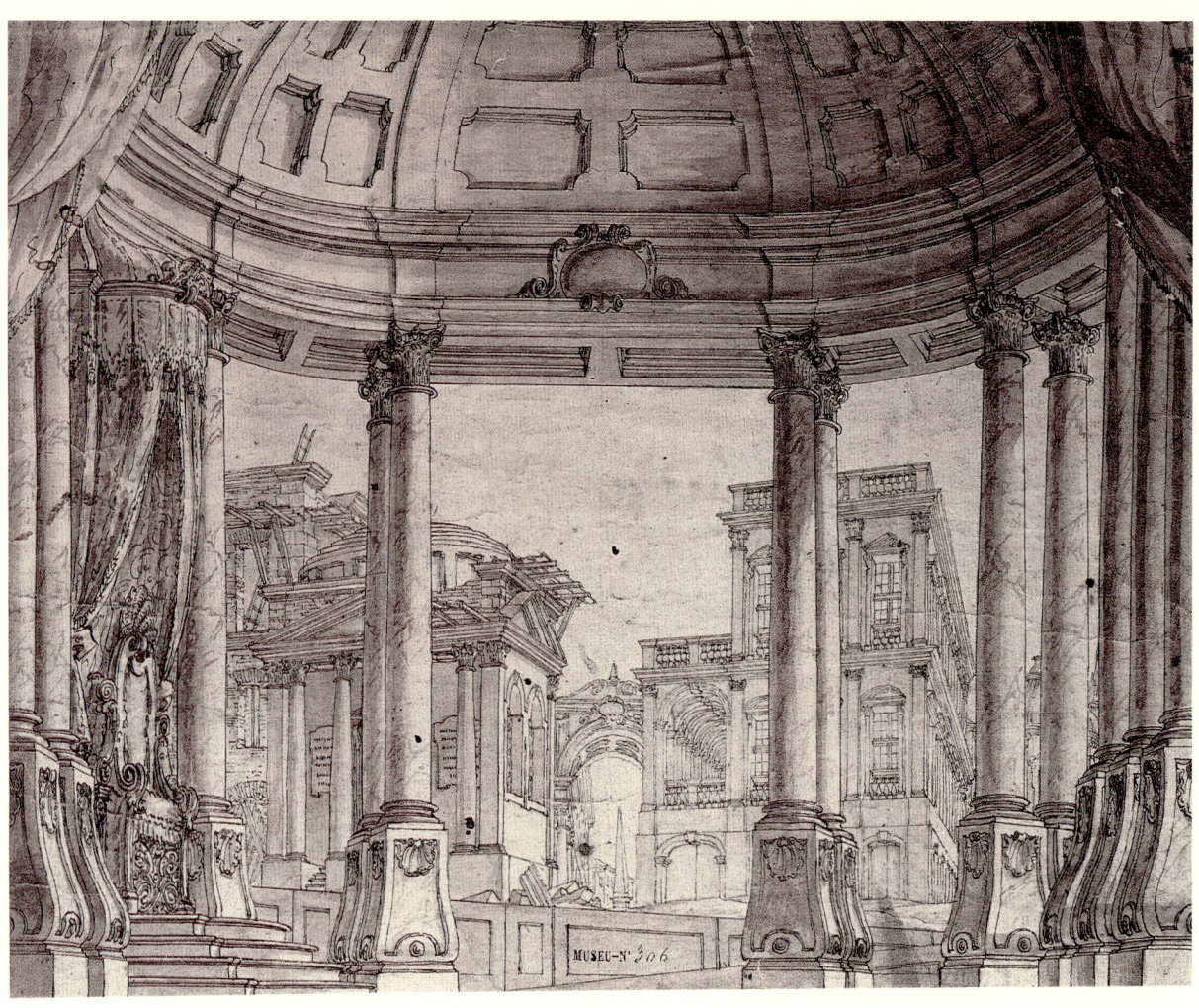

56. Giovanni Carlo Bibiena, *Royal Palace with a View of Carthage, Act 1, Scene 1*, pen and ink bistre with sepia wash

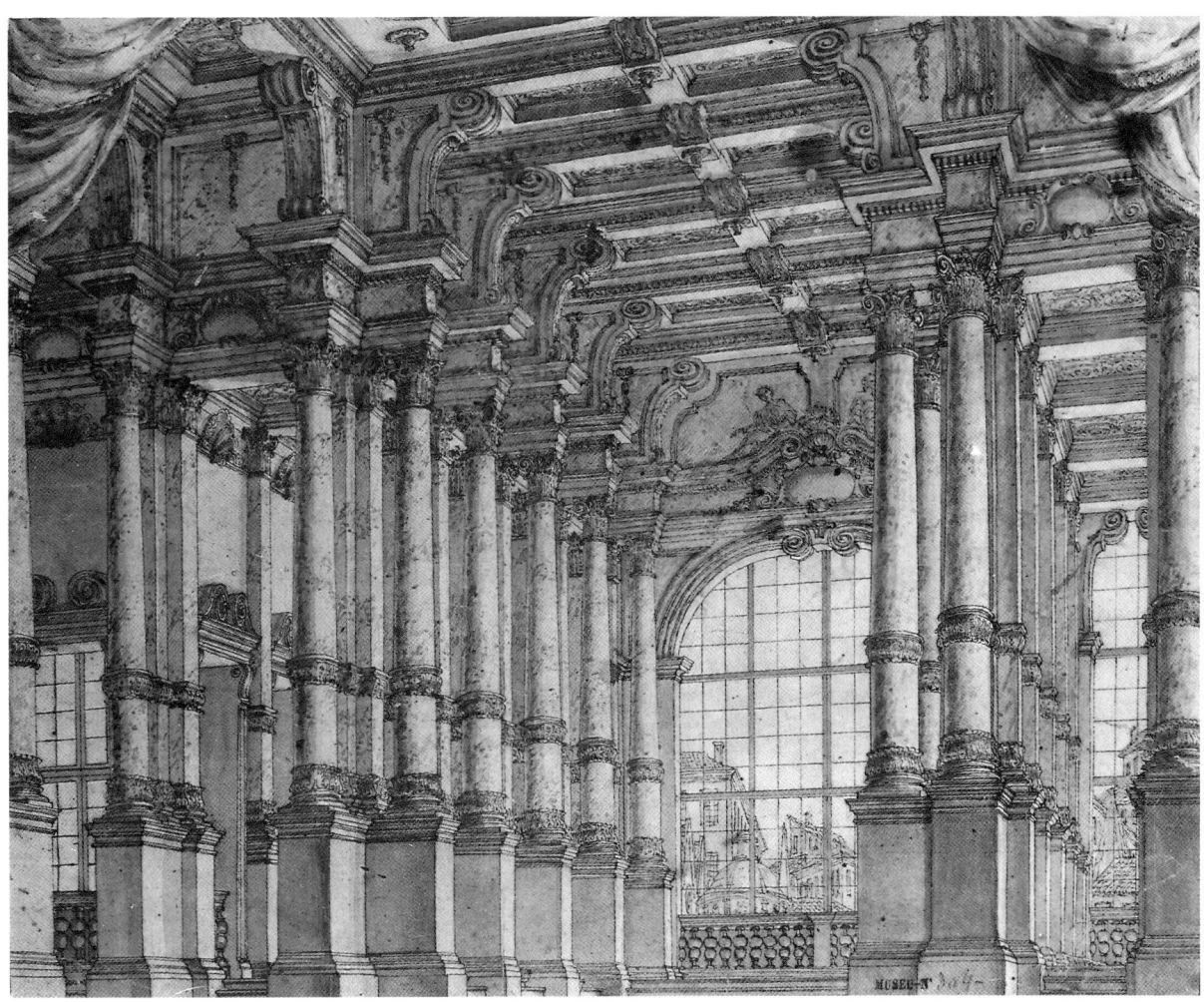

57. Giovanni Carlo Bibiena, *Royal Salon, Act 3, Scene 3*, pen and ink bistre with sepia and gray wash

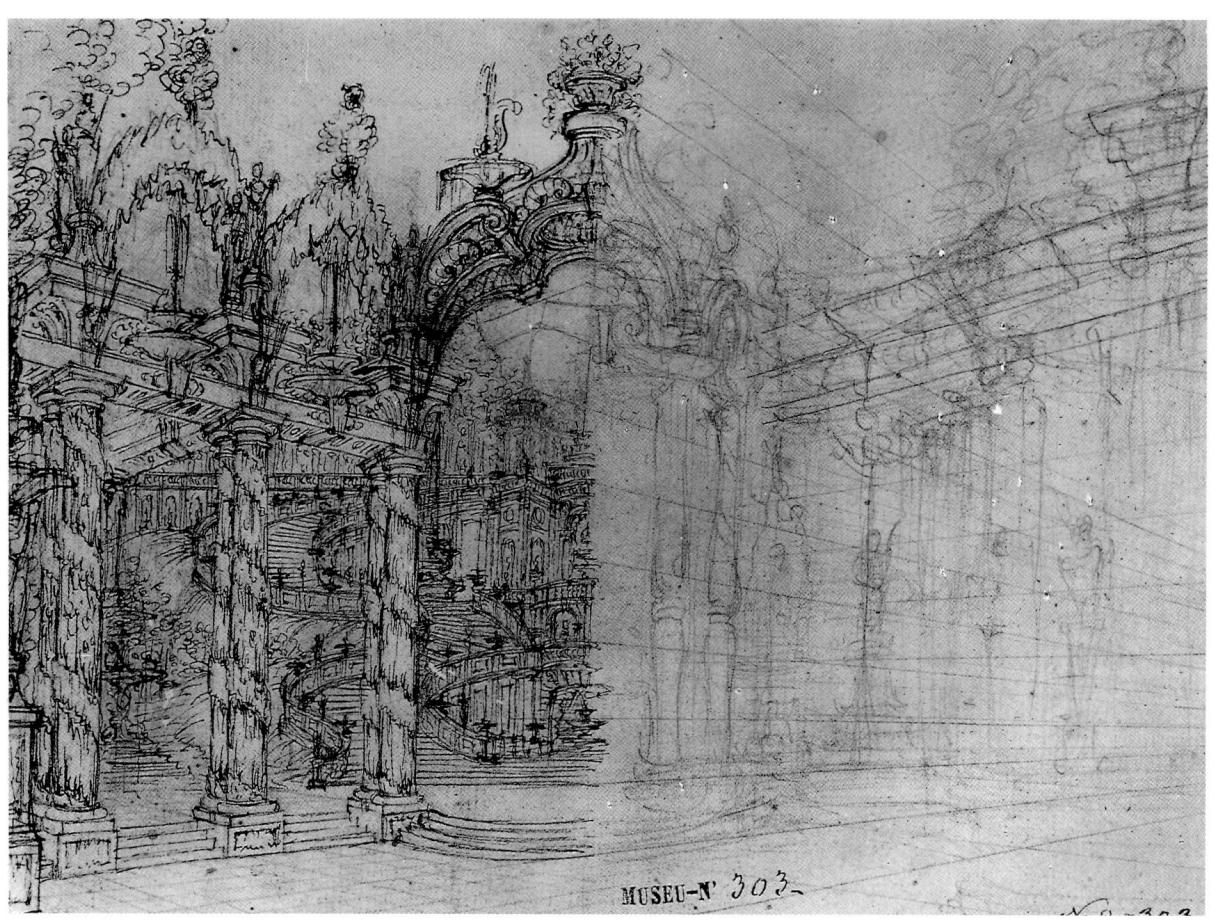

58. Giovanni Carlo Bibiena, *Study for a Stage Set, Act 1, Scene 8*, pencil, pen, and bistre

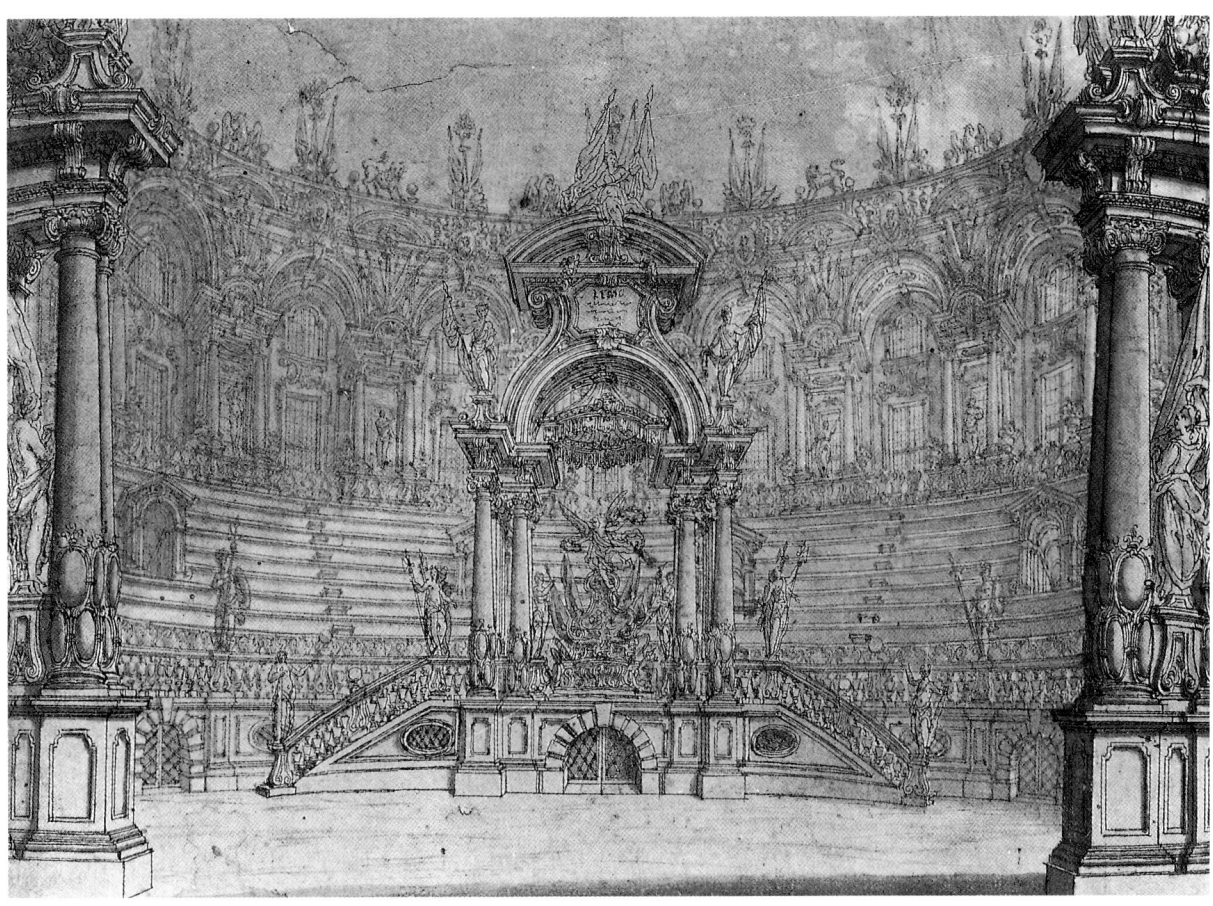

59. Giovanni Carlo Bibiena, *Amphitheater, Act 3, Scene 12*,
pencil and ink with sepia and gray wash

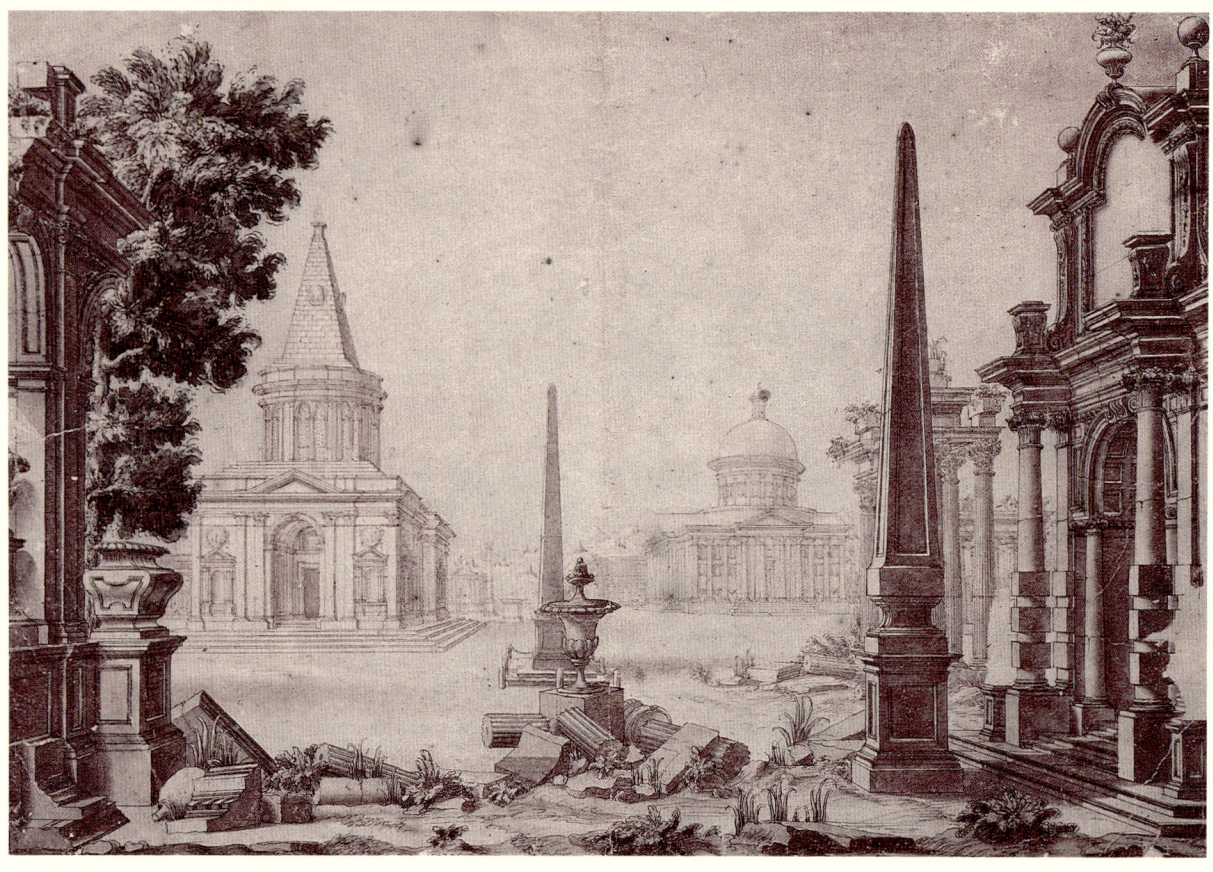

60. Giovanni Carlo Bibiena, *Opera* L'Olimpiade, *Act 2, Scene 1*, pen and ink, pencil and sepia wash

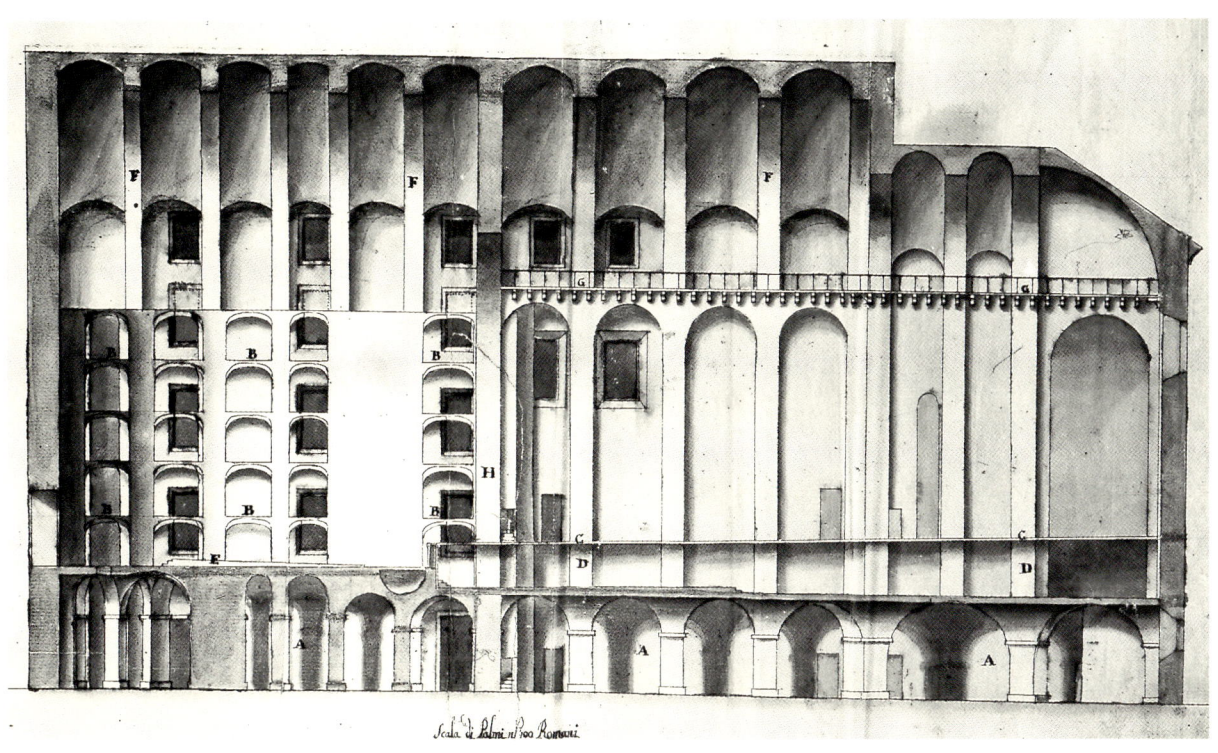

61. Giovanni Carlo Bibiena, *Longitudinal Section of a Theater*, pen with pink and gray wash

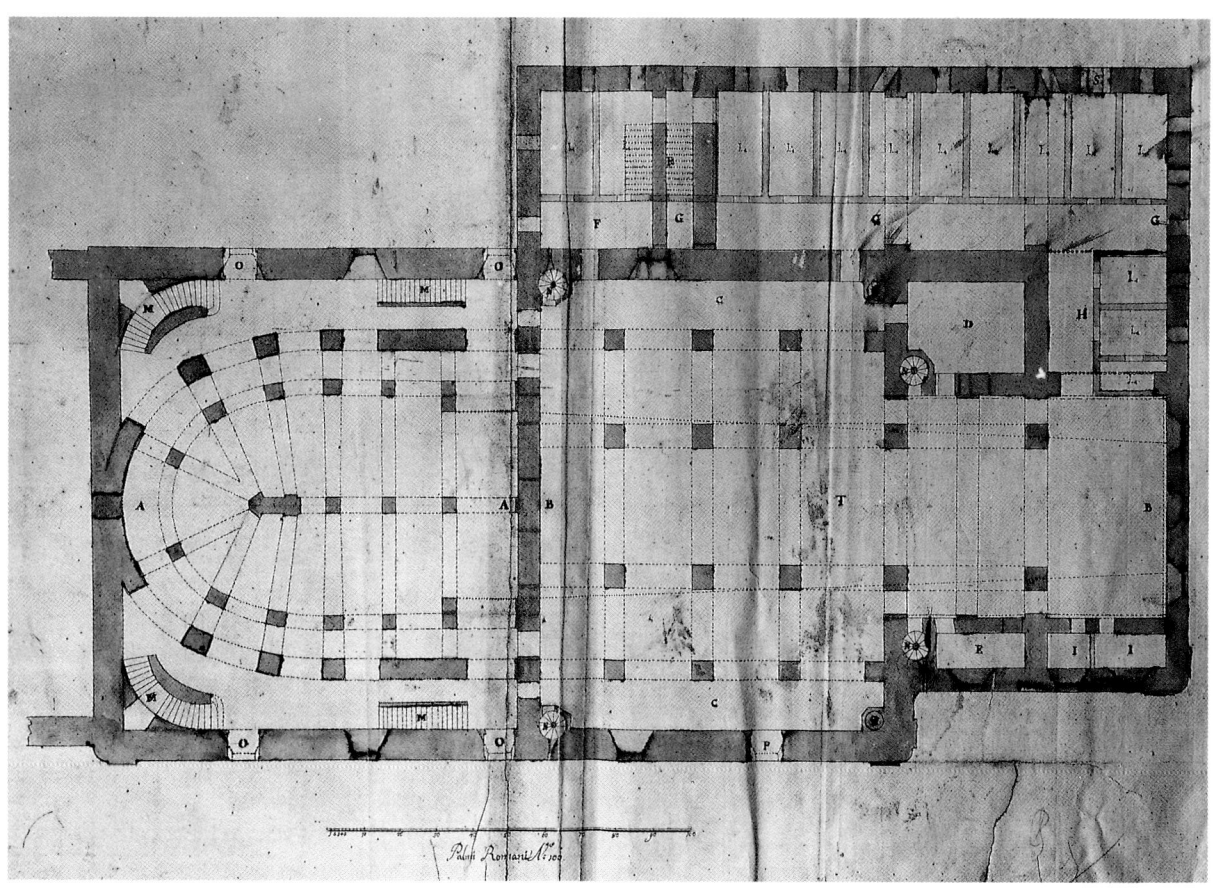

62. Giovanni Carlo Bibiena, *Plan of the Same Theater at Ground Level*, pen and ink with pink and gray wash

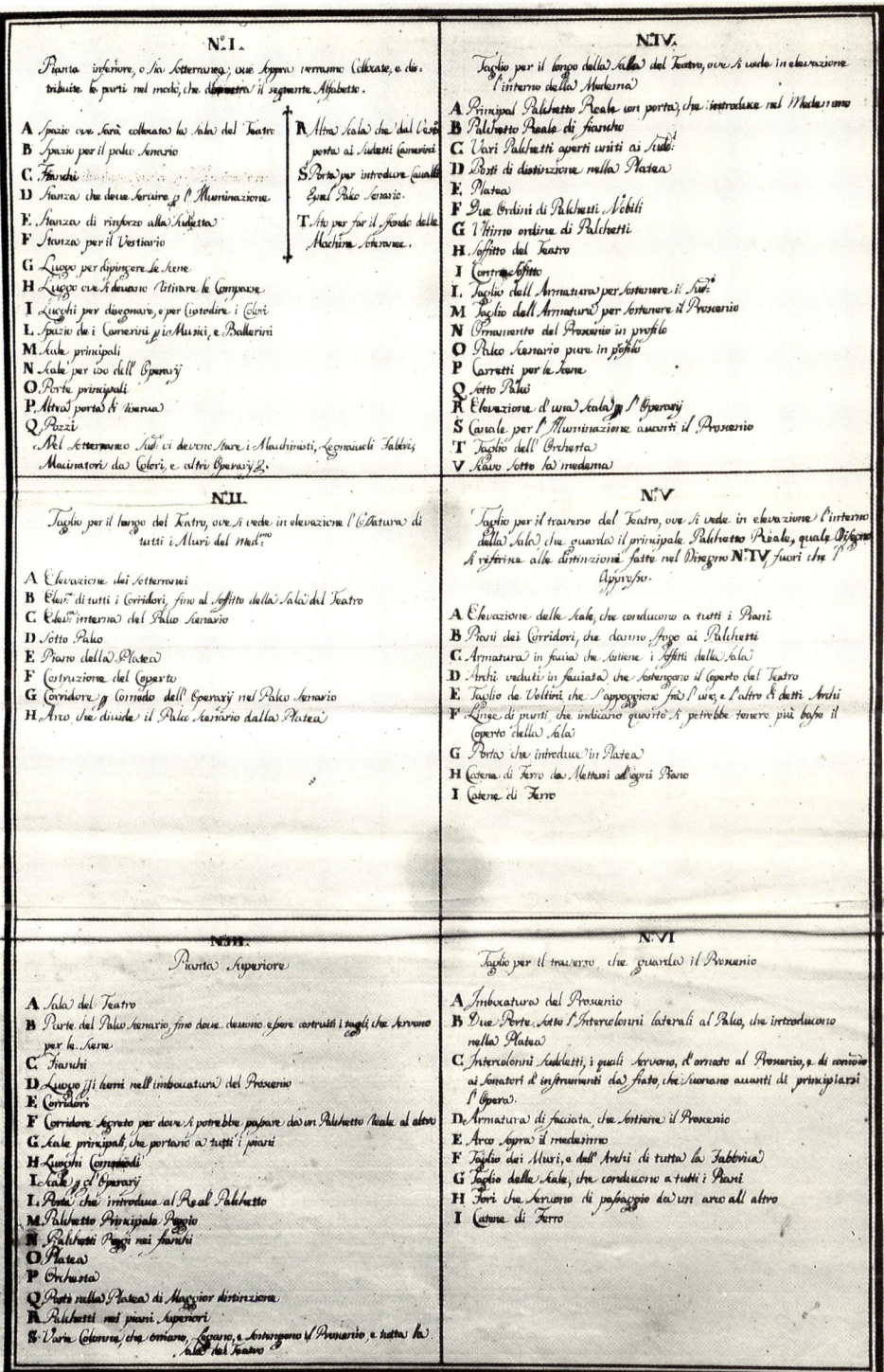

63. Giovanni Carlo Bibiena, *Descriptive Page*, pen and brown ink

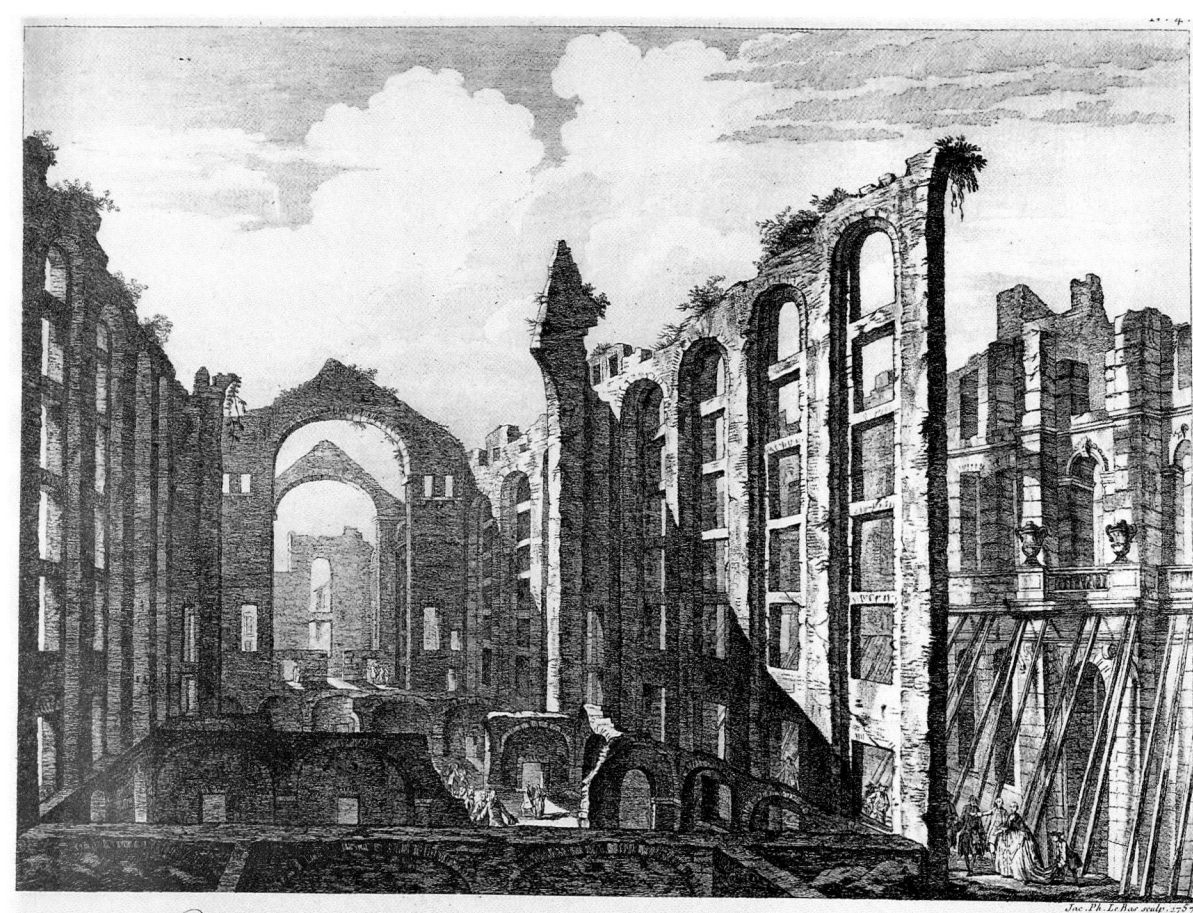

64. Jacques Philippe Le Bas, *Ruins of the Opera House after the 1755 Earthquake*, etching

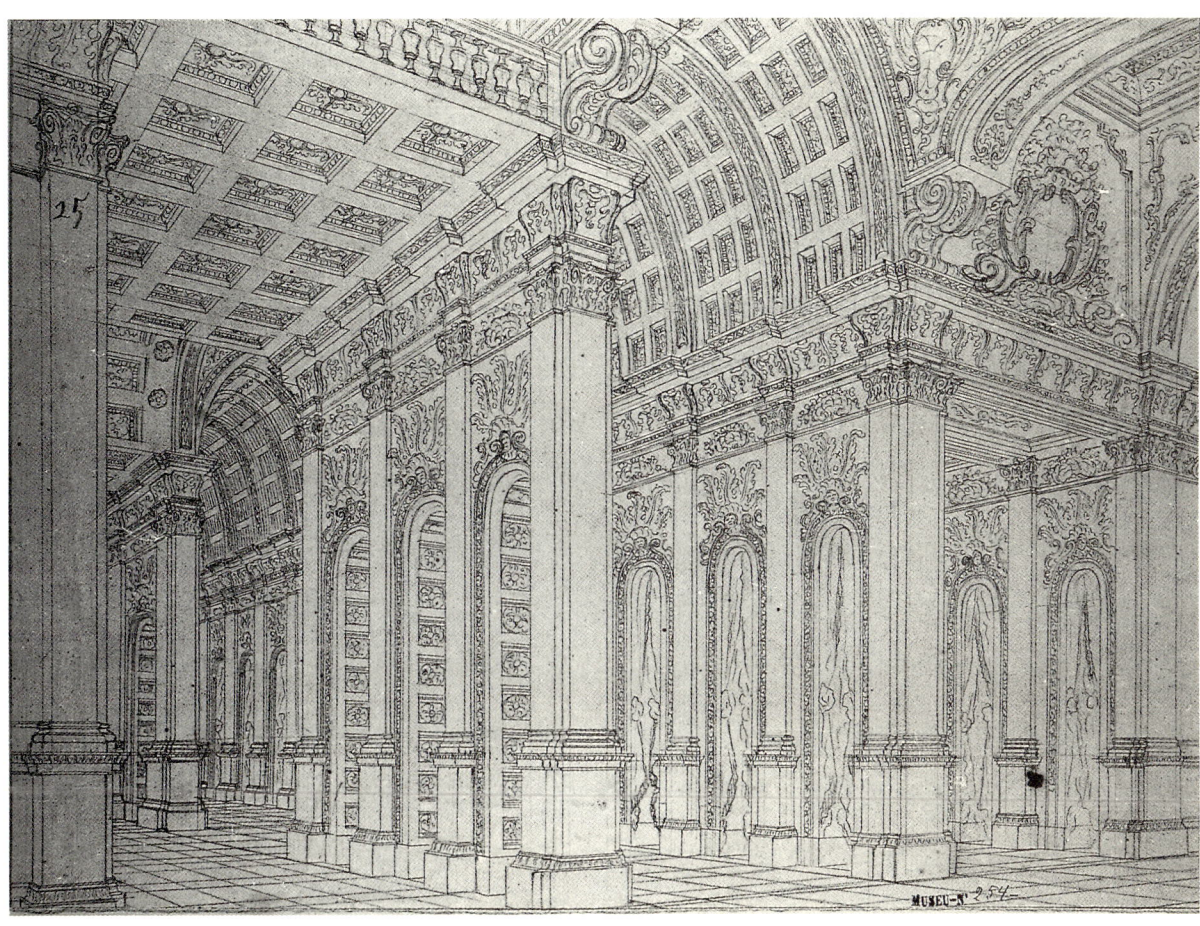

65. Bibiena School, *Stage Set of Galleries*, pencil

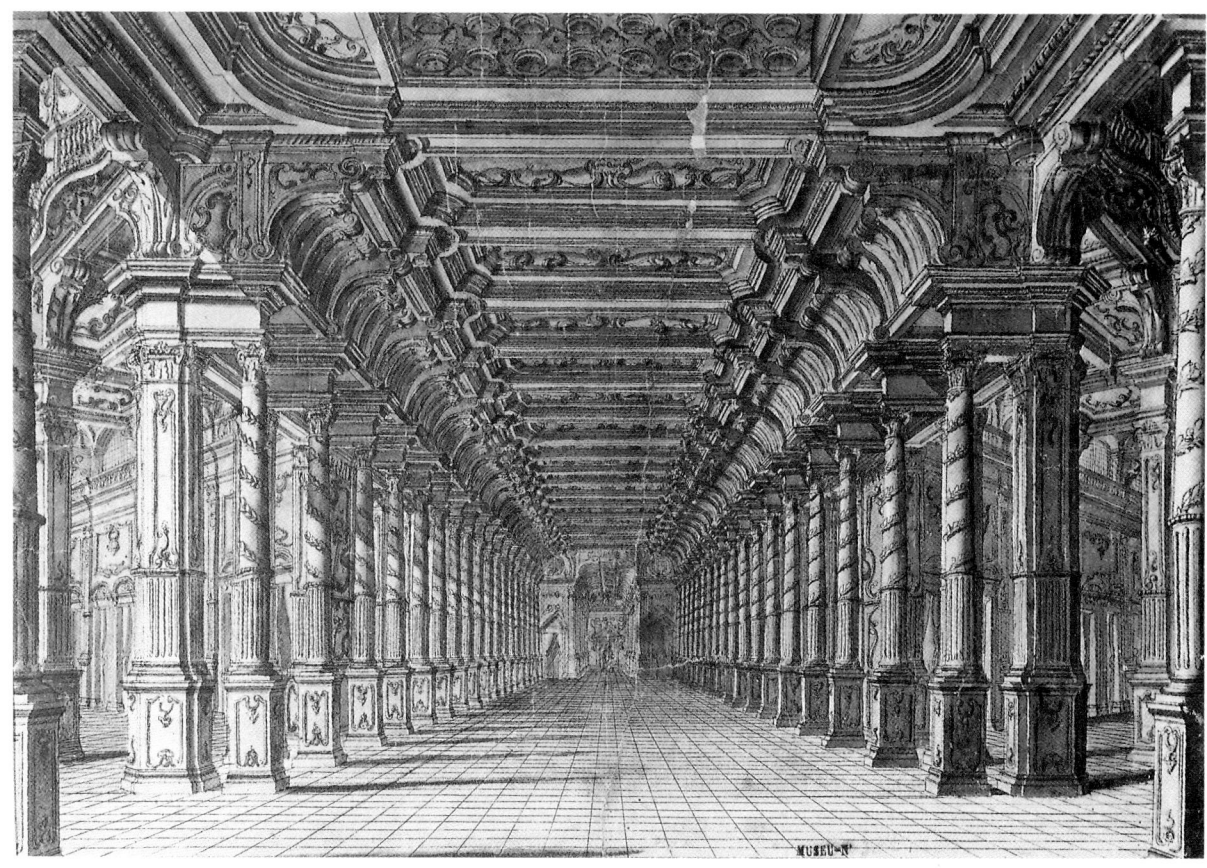

66. Bibiena School, *Background Stage Set of a Gallery*, pen and brown wash

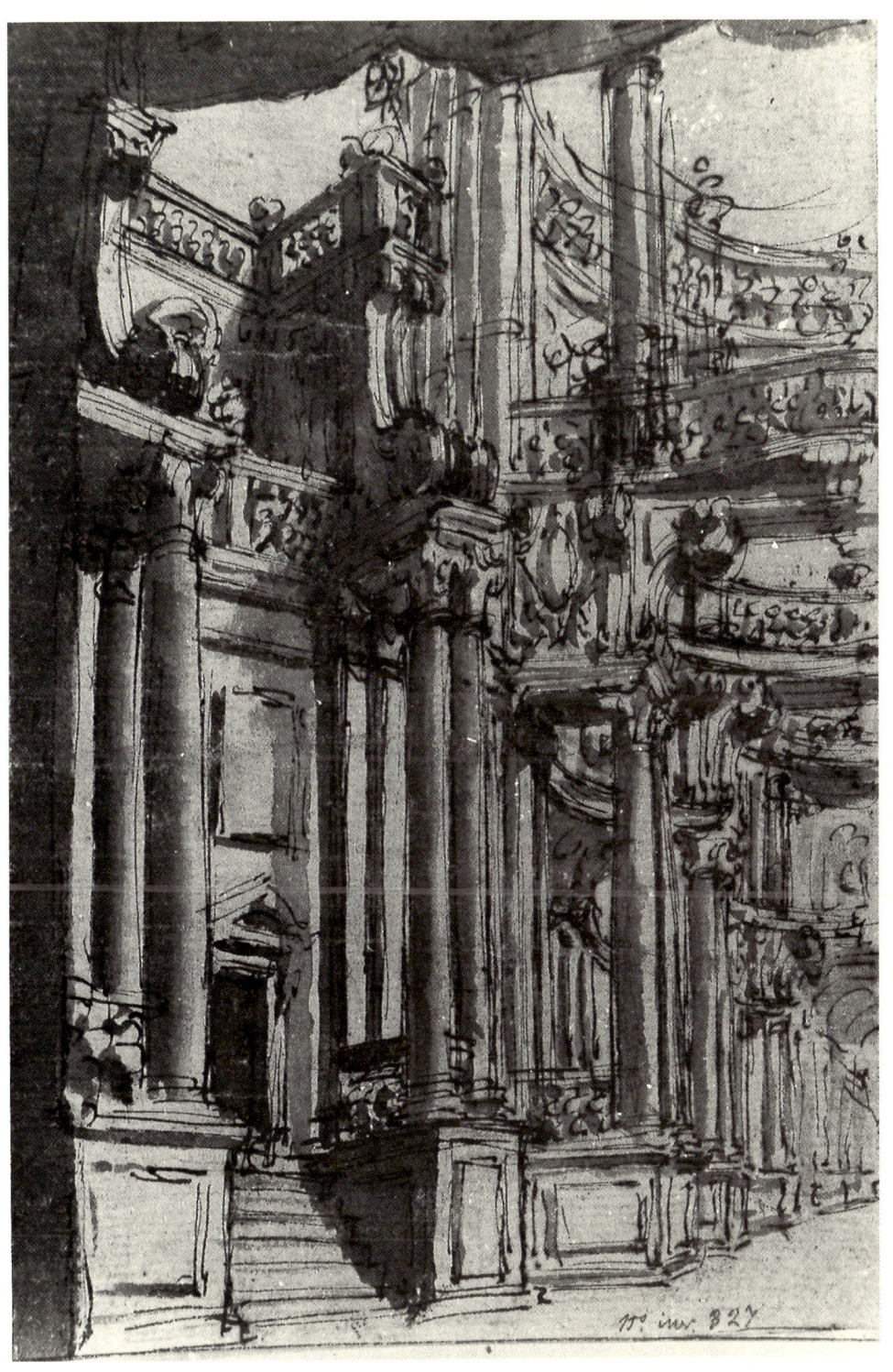

67. Bibiena School, *Draft of Architectural Stage Set*, pen and ink bistre with sepia wash

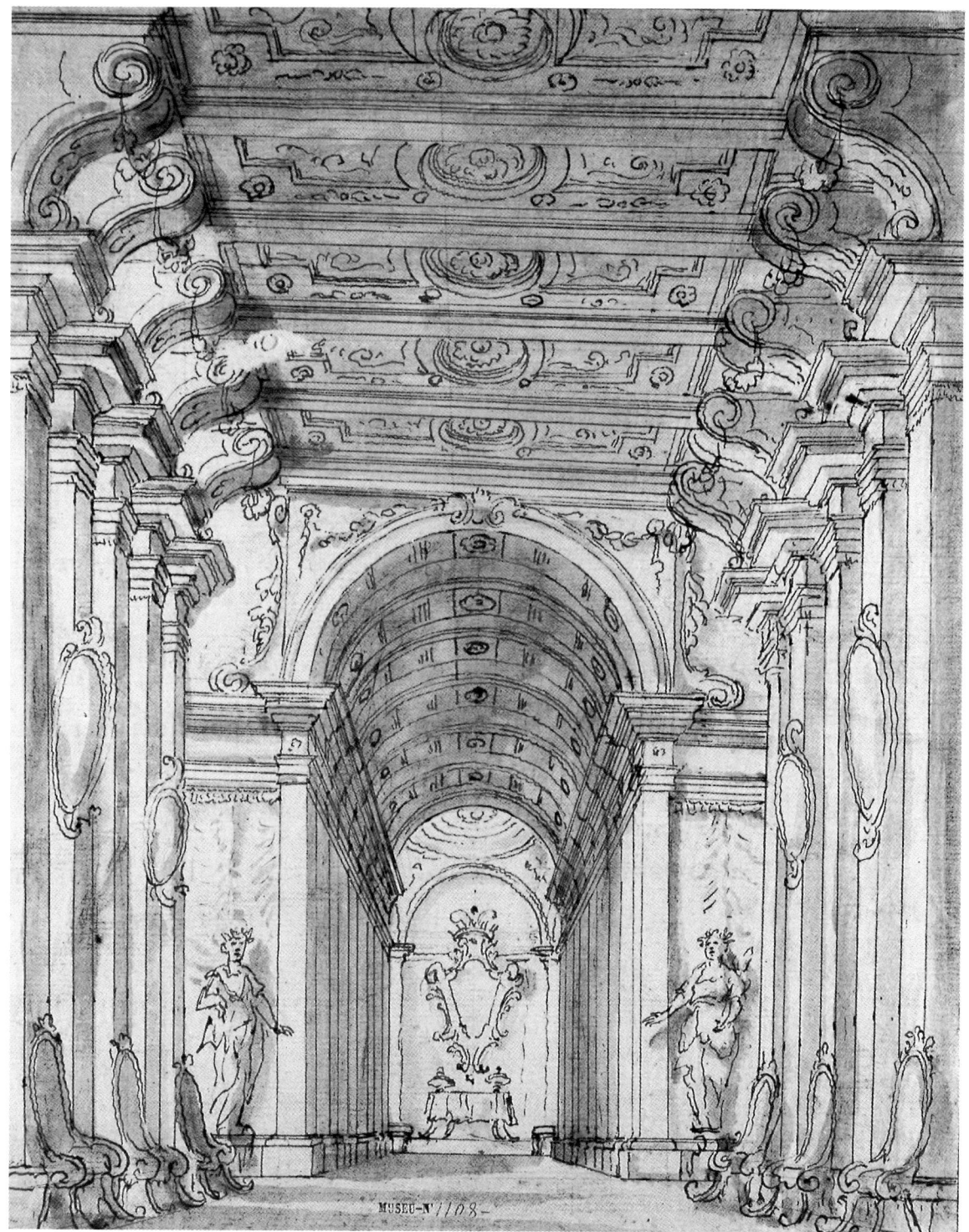

68. Bibiena School, *Stage Set of a Gallery in a Palace*, pen and ink with sepia wash

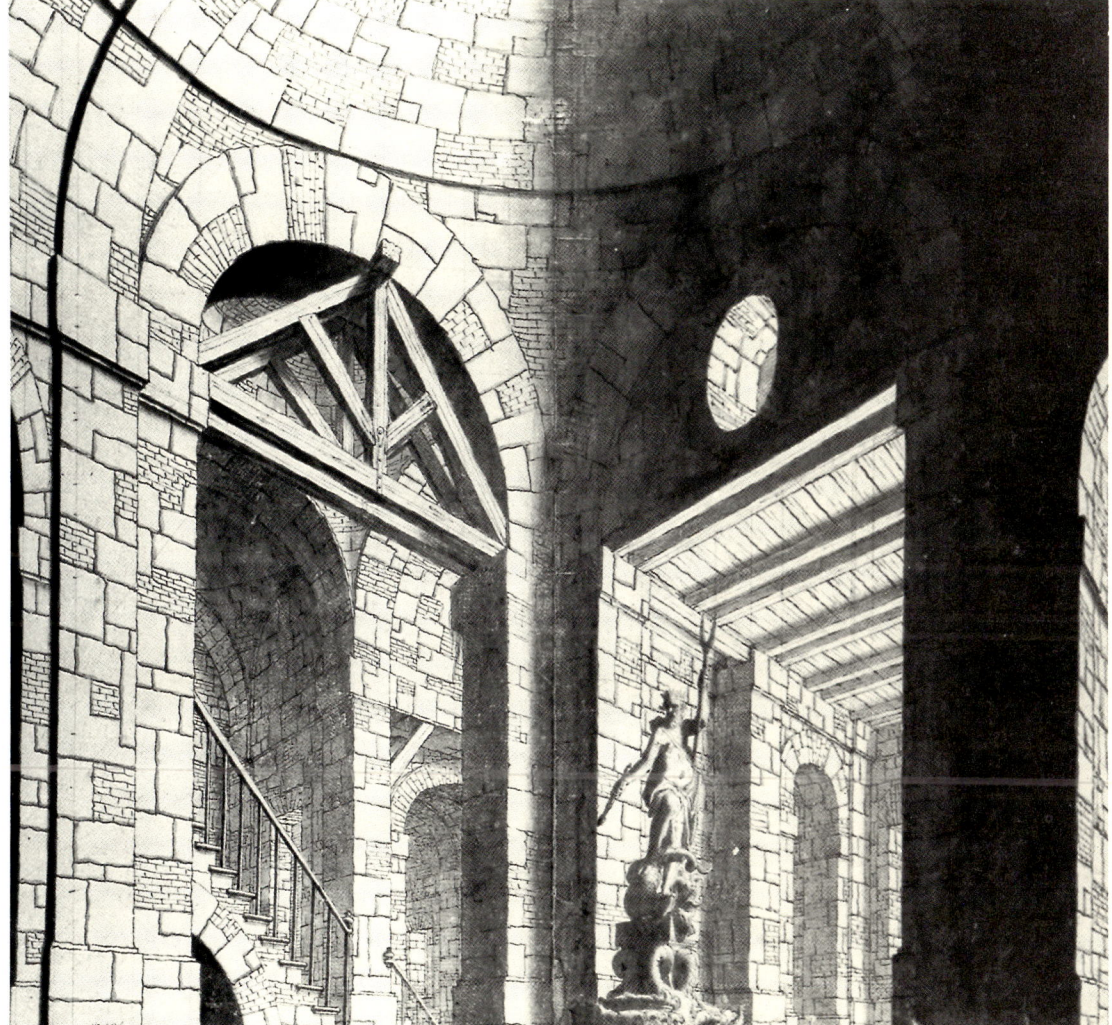

69. Bibiena School, *Interior Setting of a Fortification with a Statue of Neptune*, pen and ink with sepia wash

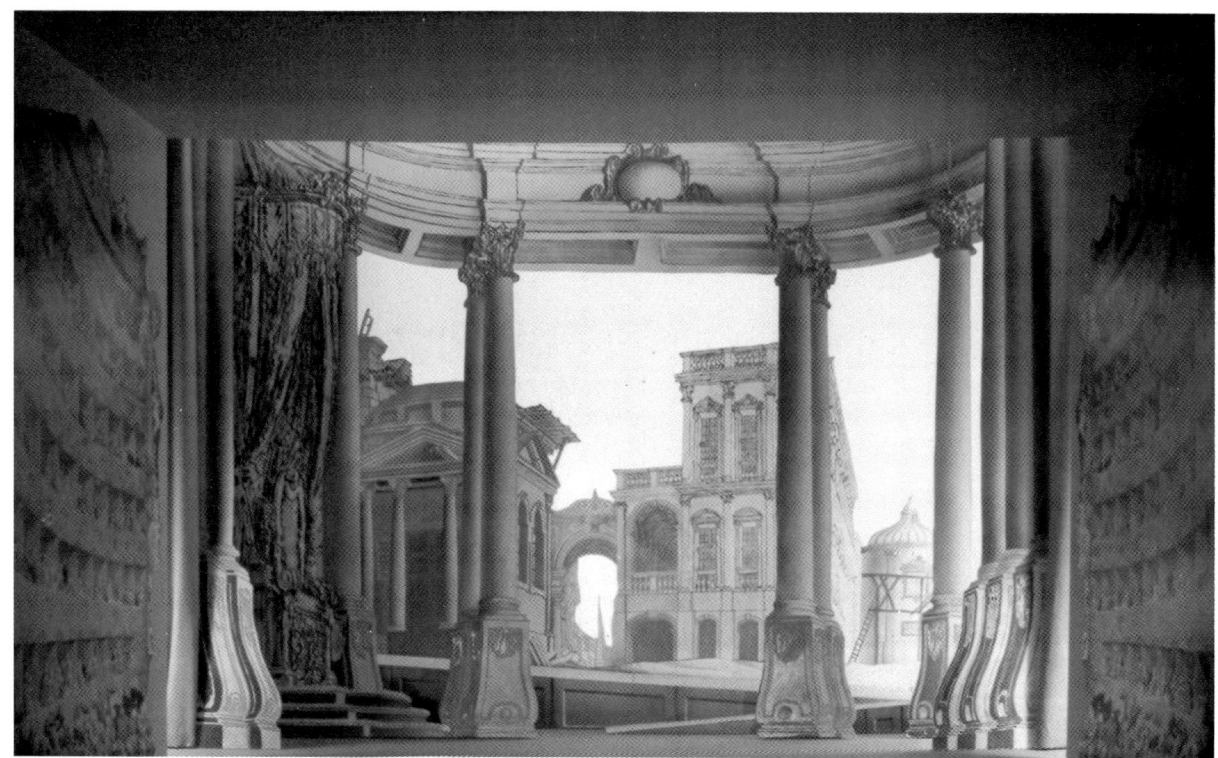

70. Model of the Royal Opera House, Lisbon; stage set based on the opera *Didone Abbandonata*

Checklist of Works

Dimensions are given in centimeters, height precedes width precedes depth. The names of lending institutions are abbreviated as follows:
MNAA = Museu Nacional de Arte Antiga
ANBA = Academia Nacional de Belas-Artes
The inventory number assigned by each museum to individual works appears after the abbreviation.

1. Martin Bernigerotti (1670–1733)
Portrait of Charles VI
Etching
32.5 x 20.5
MNAA; No. 2132p

2. Giuseppe Bibiena (1695–1757)
Study for a Stage Set
Etching
48 x 63
MNAA; No. 1291

3. Giuseppe Bibiena
Study for a Stage Set
Etching
46.5 x 53
MNAA; No. 1292

4. Giuseppe Bibiena
Study for a Stage Set
Etching
48 x 63.2
MNAA; No. 1293

5. Giuseppe Bibiena
Study for a Stage Set
Etching
41.1 x 55
MNAA; No. 1294

6. Giuseppe Bibiena
Riding School Converted into a Grand Hall
Etching
37.9 x 53.8
MNAA; No. 1295

7. Lorenzo Zucchi (1692–1764)
Architectural Study: "Expulsion of the Peddlers from the Temple"
Etching
47 x 32.5
MNAA; No. 1296

8. Ferdinando Bibiena (1657–1743)
Civil Architecture Composed with Respect to Geometry and Reduced to the Perspective and Practical Consideration of Ferdinando Galli Bibiena, Citizen of Bologna, Head Architect and Painter of Chambers and Festivals of His Majesty Charles III, Monarch of Spain, Designed and Described in Five Parts
Book
44 x 31 x 4.5
ANBA; No. 2545

9. Ferdinando Bibiena
Guide to Young Students in the Design of Civil Architecture at the Accademia Clementina of the Institute of Science. Collected by Ferdinando Galli Bibiena. First Dedicated by the Author to A.S. Cattarina de Vigri of Bologna, Protectress of the Academy. Second Edition
Book
18 x 10 x 4
ANBA; No. 1346 vol. 1

10. Ferdinando Bibiena
Guide to Young Students in the Design of Civil Architecture at the Accademia Clementina of the Institute of Science. Collected by Ferdinando Galli Bibiena. First Dedicated by the Author to A.S. Cattarina de Vigri of Bologna, Protectress of the Academy
Book
18 x 10 x 4
ANBA; No. 1346 vol. 2

11. Lorenzo Capponi (1773–?)
Plans and Analysis of the New Theater of Bologna. To the Nobleman Eminent Lord Senator Girolamo Legnani Ferri, Administrator of Justice, Admiral of the Tower of Magnavala, etc. By Lorenzo Capponi. Venice 1764
Book
42 x 30 x 1.5
ANBA; No. 1472

12. António Bibiena (?)
Plans for a Theater in Bologna
Pen and ink with gray wash
48.2 x 35.5
MNAA; No. 221

13. Francesco Bibiena (1659–1739)
Grand Atrium with Figures
Pen and ink bistre with sepia and green wash
40.6 x 57.6
MNAA; No. 308

14. Francesco Bibiena
Stage Scenery with Boats
Pen and ink with sepia wash
23.2 x 30.5
MNAA; No. 309

15. Francesco Bibiena
Grand Atrium
Pen and ink bistre with sepia wash
39.1 x 49.4
MNAA; No. 315

16. Francesco Bibiena
Interior of a Palace with Staircases
Pen and ink bistre with sepia wash
26.5 x 32.5
MNAA; No. 318

17. Francesco Bibiena
Grand Harbor with a Triumphal Arch
Pen and ink bistre with sepia wash
26.5 x 32.2
MNAA; No. 322

18. Francesco Bibiena
Grand Courtyard with Figures in the Background

Pen and ink bistre with sepia wash
33 x 46.8
MNAA; No. 321

19. Francesco Bibiena
Structures with an Obelisk as the Focal Point
Pen and ink bistre with sepia wash
26.2 x 32.1
MNAA; No. 323

20. Francesco Bibiena
Arcade of a Courtyard with a Statue of Neptune
Pen and ink bistre with sepia wash
26.4 x 32.3
MNAA; No. 325

21. Francesco Bibiena
Prison
Pen and ink with sepia wash
25.7 x 32.1
MNAA; No. 326

Opera *Fetonte*

22. Francesco Bibiena
Grand Loggia Opening onto a Garden
Pen and ink bistre with sepia wash
26.6 x 32.3
MNAA; No. 324

23. Francesco Bibiena
Theatrical Machines Used for Dance 3, Act 2, Scene 2
Pen and ink with sepia wash
34.9 x 56.6
MNAA; No. 316

24. Francesco Bibiena
Atrium of "Royal Palace of the Sun" or "The Palace of Diana," Act 3, Scene 9
Pen and ink with sepia wash
42.6 x 36.3
MNAA; No. 317

25. Francesco Bibiena
"Enchanting Royal Palace of Thetis," Act 1, Scene 2
Pen and ink bistre with sepia wash
26.4 x 32.1
MNAA; No. 319

26. Francesco Bibiena
"Enchanting Royal Palace of Thetis," Pavilion with Fountain
Pen and ink bistre with sepia wash
26.3 x 32.4
MNAA; No. 320

27. Francesco Bibiena
"Royal Palace of Diana: Symbols of the Hours," Dance 2, Act 2
Pen and ink bistre with sepia wash
44.1 x 61.5
MNAA; No. 1705

Opera *Lucio Vero, or Il Vologeso*

28. Francesco Bibiena
Amphitheater Scenery with Ostentatious Decoration
Pen and ink with sepia wash
31.5 x 28.2
MNAA; No. 310

29. Francesco Bibiena
"Grand Imperial Loggia," Act 1, Scene 1
Pen and ink with sepia wash
31.8 x 15.1
MNAA; No. 312

30. Francesco Bibiena
Portion of a Stage Design with Columns and Staircases "Per un Trionfo"
Pen and ink with sepia wash
50.5 x 31.2
MNAA; No. 313

31. Francesco Bibiena
Theater of Vienna Proscenium, Plan, and Elevation
Pen and ink, bistre, and sepia
41 x 33
MNAA; No. 224

Nancy Opera

32. Francesco Bibiena
Proscenium
Pen and ink bistre with sepia wash
31.6 x 35
MNAA; No. 314

33. Francesco Bibiena
Vertical Projections Flanking the Stage
Pen and ink bistre with sepia wash
34.2 x 56.4
MNAA; No. 219

34. Francesco Bibiena
Elevation of the Theater Boxes Facing the Stage, dated 1708
Pen and ink bistre with sepia wash
34 x 56
MNAA; No. 219A

35. Francesco Bibiena
Elevation with Four Rows of Theater Boxes
Pencil
53.2 x 35
MNAA; No. 222

36. Francesco Bibiena
Study for Theater Boxes
Pen and bistre
80.4 x 15
MNAA; No. 223

37. Francesco Bibiena
Sketch for Proscenium and Theater Boxes
Pen and ink with sepia wash
42.3 x 55.8
MNAA; No. 1705A

38. Francesco Bibiena
Part of the Bell-Shaped Ceiling with Five Rows of Theater Boxes and the Stage
Pen and ink bistre with sepia wash
35.6 x 24.4
MNAA; No. 328

39. Francesco Bibiena
Decoration for the Ceiling
Pen and ink bistre with sepia wash
49.3 x 38.8
MNAA; No. 220

Home of Francesco Bibiena in Bologna
First Project

40. Francesco Bibiena
Main Facade
Pen and ink with sepia wash
39.6 x 54.4
MNAA; No. 1676

41. Francesco Bibiena
Lateral Facade
Pen and ink with sepia wash
39.6 x 40.4
MNAA; No. 1676A

42. Francesco Bibiena
Elevations for Two Corresponding Designs
Pen and ink bistre with sepia wash
42.3 x 47
MNAA; No. 1676B

43. Francesco Bibiena
Plan Corresponding to the Lateral Facade
Pen and ink bistre with sepia wash
42.4 x 27.2
MNAA; No. 1676C

Second Project

44. Francesco Bibiena
Lateral Facade
Pen and ink bistre with sepia wash
42 x 43.7
MNAA; No. 1676D

45. Francesco Bibiena
Main Facade
Pen and ink bistre with sepia wash
42 x 47.5
MNAA; No. 1676E

46. Francesco Bibiena
Plan of the Residence with Two Corresponding Designs
Pen and ink with sepia wash
42.3 x 47
MNAA; No. 1676F

47. Francesco Bibiena
Building in Mantua
Pen and ink with sepia and pink wash
33.3 x 49
MNAA; No. 1687

48. Francesco Bibiena
Plan for Decorative Architecture
Pen and ink with sepia wash
49.3 x 51.5
MNAA; No. 272

49. Francesco Bibiena
Facade for a Palace
Pen and ink with sepia wash
30.5 x 35
MNAA; No. 286

50. Francesco Bibiena
Scenographic Composition with Symbols of the Passion of Christ
Pen and ink with sepia wash
42.6 x 36.1
MNAA; No. 189

51. Francesco Bibiena
Composition for an Altarpiece Alluding to Death
Pen and ink with sepia wash
47.9 x 36.1
MNAA; No. 190

52. Francesco Bibiena
Project for an Altar Elevation
Pen and ink with sepia wash
47.9 x 30.5
MNAA; No. 246

53. Francesco Bibiena
Elevation and Plan for an Altar with the Image of a Pious Saint
Pen and ink with greenish brown wash
88.3 x 34.5
MNAA; No. 433

54. Francesco Bibiena
Elevation and Plan for an Altar with the Image of Our Lady of the Assumption
Pen and ink with brown and greenish gray wash
57 x 32.5
MNAA; No. 252

55. Francesco Bibiena
Elevation and Plan for an Altar of the Church of the Holy Spirit in Bologna
Pen and ink with sepia wash
86.7 x 41.5
MNAA; No. 1650

Opera *Didone Abbandonata*

56. Giovanni Carlo Bibiena (1717–1760)
Royal Palace with a View of Carthage, Act 1, Scene 1
Pen and ink bistre with sepia wash
27.7 x 34.8
MNAA; No. 306

57. Giovanni Carlo Bibiena
Royal Salon, Act 3, Scene 3
Pen and ink bistre with sepia and gray wash
27.8 x 34.8
MNAA; No. 304

Opera *Clemenza di Tito*, performed in the Royal Opera House on 6 June 1755 to celebrate the birthday of King Joseph I

58. Giovanni Carlo Bibiena
Study for a Stage Set, Act 1, Scene 8
Pencil, pen, and bistre
15.2 x 21.7
MNAA; No. 303

59. Giovanni Carlo Bibiena
Amphitheater, Act 3, Scene 12
Pencil and ink with sepia and gray wash
16.7 x 23.4
MNAA; No. 311

60. Giovanni Carlo Bibiena
Opera L'Olimpiade, Act 2, Scene 1
Pen and ink, pencil and sepia wash
32.1 x 46.6
MNAA; No. 305

Royal Opera House, 1755

61. Giovanni Carlo Bibiena
Longitudinal Section of a Theater
Pen with pink and gray wash
44.5 x 59.9
ANBA

62. Giovanni Carlo Bibiena
Plan of the Same Theater at Ground Level
Pen and ink with pink and gray wash
45.2 x 60.8
ANBA

63. Giovanni Carlo Bibiena
Descriptive Page
Pen and brown ink
45.2 x 60.8
ANBA

64. Jacques Philippe Le Bas (1707–1783)
Ruins of the Opera House after the 1755 Earthquake
Etching
37 x 55
MNAA; No. 915

65. Bibiena School
Stage Set of Galleries
Pencil
24.7 x 35
MNAA; No. 254

66. Bibiena School
Background Stage Set of a Gallery
Pen and brown wash
34.9 x 36.9
MNAA; No. 307

67. Bibiena School
Draft of Architectural Stage Set
Pen and ink bistre with sepia wash
14.3 x 9.7
MNAA; No. 327

68. Bibiena School
Stage Set of a Gallery in a Palace
Pen and ink with sepia wash
37 x 29.6
MNAA; No. 1108

69. Bibiena School
Interior Setting of a Fortification with a Statue of Neptune
Pen and ink with sepia wash
39 x 43
MNAA; No. 196

70. Model of the Royal Opera House, Lisbon
Stage set based on the opera *Didone Abbandonata*
Wood, photographs, fabric, paint
49 x 78 x 41
MNAA

Bibliography

Antoine, Michel. "L'Opéra de Nancy." *Le Pays Lorrain* 46, no. 1 (1965): 1–23.

ARCHITETTURE, E PROSPETIVE / DEDICATE / ALLA MAESTA / DI / CARLO SESTO / IMPERADOR DE ROMANI / DA / GIUSEPPE GALLI BIBIENA, / SUO PRIMO INGEGNER TEATRALE, ED ARCHITETTO, / INVENTORE DELLE MEDESINE / AUGUSTA / Sotto la Direzione di Andrea Pfeffel / MDCCXL. With an introduction by A. Hyatt Mayor. New York: Dover Publications, Inc., 1964.

Beaumont, Maria Alice. "Arquitectura e cenografia nos desenhos dos Galli Bibiena." *Revista S. Carlos*, no. 5 (July–Oct. 1987): 12–15.

———. "Stage Sets by the Bibienas in the Museu Nacional de Arte Antiga, Lisbon." *Apollo*, no. 134 (April 1973): 408–15.

Benois, Nicola. "L'art de la Scénographie." *Le Livre de Jours Italiens: Le Theatre lyrique.* Année 12. Rome: Office National Italien de Tourisme, 1963.

Carvalho, Ayres de. *Catálogo da Colecção de Desenhos.* Lisbon: Biblioteca Nacional, 1977.

———. *Os Três Arquitectos da Ajuda: do Rocaille ao Neoclássico.* Lisbon: Direcção-Geral do Património Cultural, 1979.

Castelo-Branco, Camilo. *Noites de Insónia.* Porto: E. Chardron, 1847.

Castilho, Júlio de. *A Ribeira de Lisboa.* Vol. 3. Lisbon: Câmara Municipal, 1941.

———. *Lisboa Antiga.* Vol. 5. Lisbon: Livraria Ferreira, 1902.

Catálogo da Colecção de Desenhos do Museu Nacional de Bellas-Artes. Lisbon: Imprensa Nacional, 1905.

Collier, W. "Rediscovered Theatre Drawing by António Bibiena." *Apollo* (1967): 108–11.

Correia, Joaquim Manuel da Silva. "Teatros Régios do séc. XVIII." *Boletim do Museu Nacional de Arte Antiga* 5, nos. 3 and 4 (1969): 24–38.

Correia, Joaquim Manuel da Silva, and Natália Brito Correia Guedes. *O Paço Real de Salvaterra de Magos. A Corte. A Ópera. A Falcoaria.* Lisbon: Livros Horizonte, 1989.

Costa, Luís Xavier da. *As Belas-Artes Plásticas em Portugal durante o séc. XVIII.* Lisbon: J. Rodrigues, 1934.

David Peres e a sua Época 1711–1778: Catálogo da exposição. Lisbon: Biblioteca Nacional, 1979.

Desenhos Italianos: Catálogo da 18ª exposição temporária. Lisbon: Museu Nacional de Arte Antiga, 1958.

Desenhos Italianos do séc. XVIII (Escola dos Bibiena): Catálogo da exposição temporária. Lisbon: Museu Nacional de Arte Antiga, 1964.

Dias, João Pereira. *Cenários do Teatro de S. Carlos.* Lisbon: Bertrand (Irmãos), 1940.

———. "La Scénographie Baroque au Portugal." *XVI Congrès International d'Histoire de l'Art.* Vol. 2. Lisbon-Porto (1949): 328–32.

Ferrero, Mercedes Viale. "Disegn Scenografici per opere Sartiane." *Giuseppe Sarti Musicista Faentino—Atti convegno internazionale.* Faenza (November 1983): 173–92.

Figueiredo, José de. "Teatro Real da Ópera." *Boletim da Academia Nacional de Belas-Artes* 3 (1941): 33–35.

Figueiredo, Manuel de. *Teatro.* Vol. 14. Lisbon: n.p., 1815.

França, José Augusto. *Lisboa Pombalina e o Iluminismo.* Lisbon: Livros Horizonte, 1966.

Lavagnino, Emilio. *Opera del Genio Italiano All'Estereo.* Vol. 1 of *Gli artisti Italian in Portogallo.* Rome: La Libreria dello Stato, 1940.

Machado, Cirillo Wolkmar. *Colecção de Memórias relativas às vidas dos pintores e escultores, arquitectos e gravadores portugueses e dos estrangeiros que estiverão em Portugal.* Lisbon: Imprensa de Victoriano Rodrigues da Silva, 1823.

Mancini, Franco. *Scenografia italiana dal Rinascimento all'etá romantica.* Milan: Fratelli Fabri Editori, 1966.

Mancini, Franco, et al. *Illusione e pratica teatrale: proposte per una lettura dello spazio scenico dagli Intermedi fiorentini all'Opera comica veneziana. Catalogo della Mostra.* Venice: Neri Pozza Editore, 1975.

Mariani, Valerio. *Storia della Scenografia Italiana.* Florence: Rinascimento del Libro, 1930.

Matteuci, Ana Maria, et al. *Architettura, Scenografia Pittura di paesaggio. Catálogo da X Biennale d'Arte Antica: L'Art del Settecento Emiliano. Museu Civico 8 Settembre–25 Novembre 1979.* Bologna: Edizioni Alfa, 1980.

Matos Sequeira, Gustavo. *Teatro de Outros Tempos: Elementos para a história do Teatro Português.* Lisbon: n.p., 1933.

―――. "Velhos Teatros de Lisboa Desaparecida." *Olisipo* 15, no. 58 (April 1958): 70–78.

Mayor, A. Hyatt. *The Bibiena Family.* New York: M. Bittner and Company, 1945.

McClymonds, Marita. *Niccolo Jommele: The Last Years, Part I.* University Microfilms International, 1979.

Muraro, Maria Teresa, and Elena Povoledo. *Disegni Teatrali dei Bibiena.* Venice: Neri Pozza Editore, 1970.

Paganuzzi, Saggi di E., et al. *L'Accademia Filarmonica di Verona e il Suo Teatro.* Verona: Accademia Filarmonica di Verona, 1982.

Pariset, François-Georges. "L'Opera de Nancy de François Bibiena (1708–1709)." *Urbanisme et Architecture: Études, écrites, et publiées en l'honneur de Pierre Lavedan.* Paris: n.p., 1954.

Rava, Carlo Enrico. *Scenografie del Museo Teatrale alla Scala dal XVI al XIX Secolo. Catalogo della Mostra.* Venice: Neri Pozza Editore, 1965.

Ribeiro, Mário Sampayo. "À margem da Exposição de Desenhos da Escola dos Bibiena." *Boletim do Museu Nacional de Arte Antiga* 5, no. 2 (1966): 26–31.

Santos, Vitor Pavão dos. "A Ópera do Tejo." *Revista Histórica* 8 (June 1979): 18–27.

Sasportes, José. *História da Dança em Portugal.* Lisbon: Fundação Calouste Gulbenkian, 1970.

Silva, Augusto Vieira da. *As freguesias de Lisboa.* Lisbon: Câmara Municipal, 1934.

―――. *As Muralhas da Ribeira de Lisboa.* vol. 1., 2d ed. Lisbon: Câmara Municipal, 1941.

Soares, Ernesto. "David Perez (subsidios para a sua biografia)." *Feira da Ladra* 6, no. 6 (1934): 205–22.

Sousa, Viterbo. *Diccionario historico e documental dos Architectos, Engenheiros e Construtores Portugueses ou a Serviço de Portugal.* Lisbon: Imprensa Nacional, 1899.

Zecchinato, A. *Il Teatro Filarmonico di Verona.* Verona: n.p., 1956.

Library of Congress Cataloging-in-Publication Data

Beaumont, Maria Alice Mourisca.
  Eighteenth-Century scenic and architectural design : drawings by the
  Galli Bibiena Family from collections in Portugal /
  Maria Alice Beaumont.
      p.   cm.
  Includes bibliographical references.
  ISBN 0-88397-094-5
  1. Bibiena, Francesco, 1659–1739—Exhibitions.   2. Bibiena,
Giovanni Carlo, 1717–1760—Exhibitions.   3. Architectural
drawing—17th century—Italy—Exhibitions.   4. Architectural
drawing—18th century—Italy—Exhibitions.   5. Theaters—Europe—
Construction—Exhibitions.   6. Theaters—Europe—Stage-setting and
scenery—Exhibitions.   7. Architectural drawing—Portugal—
Exhibitions.   I. Art Services International.   II. Title.
NA2707.B54A4   1990
792'.025' 0922—dc20   90-33939
                                                                     CIP

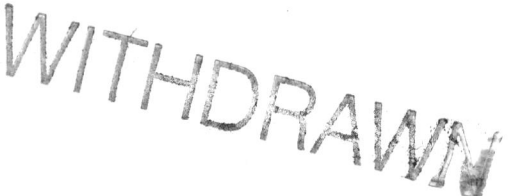